Praise for Follow the Leader

"Stephanie has always been a big advocate for women being more involved in the political realm. Follow the Leader is a must-read for anyone interested in getting an inside view on the political process and her personal journey to get where she is today."

-Attorney Benjamin Crump, Esq., Noted Civil Rights Attorney

Follow the Leader

Stephanie Mickle

13th & Joan books may be purchased for educational, business or sales promotional use. For information, please email the Sales Department at sales@13thandjoan.com.

Printed in the U.S. A.
First Printing, August 2018
Library of Congress Cataloging-in-Publication Data has been applied for.
ISBN 978-1-7324712-0-7

Dedication

THIS BOOK IS dedicated to my beloved Grandfather, Daddy Mick, who is somewhere reading it from beyond the Pearly Gates. I thank you for everything you taught me about politics, leadership, and life. I miss you, and I hope that I can become everything that you believed that I could be.

Foreword

I BECAME A judge when Stephanie was seven years old, after practicing law for a number of years and teaching law at the University of Florida. Although Stephanie did not quite know what a judge did at that age, she knew I wore business attire every day to an office. She knew my judicial assistant wore business attire every day to an office, and she knew she wanted to wear business attire and go to an office one day. In her mind, she thought that doing so was one indicator of someone doing important and impactful things in life.

I would often tell lawyers and other legal professionals, "if you think that I am impressive, then you should meet my daughter!" Stephanie would often accompany me to work functions from the time that she was eleven years old, and she would see those lawyers towering over her as a little girl. Many times, she was the only child in the room. Of course, I was so proud of her and did not want her to ever be overlooked.

When her friends were playing with dolls and other typical little girl pursuits, she was intellectually curious about how she could do important and impactful things in life. She would do the same with my father, who was a community leader and democratic, block captain. She still does so today when she meets people from whom she believes that she can learn. Even though she is most accomplished in her own right, Stephanie is, in a word, unique in that way.

She is and always has been committed to the lifelong pursuit of knowledge and taking actions that she believes are important and impactful. As her father, I have always done my best to support her, even in those times that others may not have understood her path or her decisions.

Being a judge for thirty-five years, with the last sixteen years as a federal judge, I have faced many important decisions encompassing matters of life, death, family, domestic proportions and others involving issues of constitutional importance. I believe that the decision to engage in the political process is another important decision for each citizen to face.

The human spirit has an incredible ability to overcome and to seek what is right or what is best, but making that happen requires a path to follow. In the law, we call it legal precedence; in faith, we call it the Bible or other doctrinal text, or a moral compass.

Follow the Leader offers one path to women and men. To those who may not have been involved in politics in the past but are now ready and interested to learn more about the political process, it explains why our unique voices matter to the important discussions of governance taking place across our country. It shares an inside look at the personal experiences of one woman, my daughter, Stephanie.

I encourage you to read this book from that perspective and embrace the information it contains. Glean from it the specific lessons that will help you in your own decision-making process.

Stephan P. Mickle, Sr.
Retired Senior Judge, U.S. Northern District of Florida

Preface:
Moving Beyond the March

On January 16, 2017, I wrote the following:

I WOKE UP Monday morning, thinking about going downtown to participate in my local community Martin Luther King Day celebration activities. This included a day filled with recognizing scholarship award recipients, making, and listening to speeches, and participating in a commemorative march in honor of Dr. King. This sounds good, but just the day before, I had attended an event sponsored by my sorority in honor of our Founder's Day. I found myself in a conversation with a sorority sister about the frustrating lack of progress in our communities. It became increasingly tiresome for me to hear the same old concerns about economic and educational disparities on one side of town versus another. It had become increasingly frustrating to be a part of discussions about my political party, the democratic party, being completely out of touch with its base and ultimately out of office because we failed to make the necessary adjustments. We, therefore, were not responsive to the concerns of citizens over the last two midterm elections and during the 2016 Presidential Election. I lamented aloud the following:

"Why is it acceptable to stay in pain? Is it okay not to move when the cheese has moved? When will we stop and confront the fact that what we have been doing is not working?" The definition of insanity is continuing to repeat the same thing, but expecting a different outcome. In some ways, this is what we are doing as African Americans.

So -- while I did put on my black Martin Luther King and Obama commemorative t-shirt, and while I did post something in my social media stream that wished everyone a "Happy Martin Luther King Day", accompanied by a video of Dr. King's most famous quotes on Monday -- I decided instead to spend some time penning these concerns which weigh heavily on my heart. These are concerns that I believe Dr. Martin Luther King and President Barack Obama would have also espoused and tracked for the nation.

We have come to the end of the most historic presidency in our time. President Barack Hussein Obama, the first African American President, will be heralded as one of the greatest Presidents of all times in the history of the United States of America. The end of his presidency has ushered in a time when we are seeing the long overdue recognition of the skills of more and more African American Oscar and Golden Globe winners. Positive television images frequently celebrate the phenomenal accomplishments of women athletes like Simone Biles and Serena Williams. We are marveling in the intellectual brilliance and scientific acumen of people like Neil Tyson DeGrasse and Katherine Johnson. Why don't we or why can't we, do more to realize actual change and see tangible improvements in African American communities across this country?

I know first-hand from working at the highest levels of government and in the advancement of public policy for over twenty years, that change is hard, slow and most times incremental. It requires an iron will, and sometimes a steel fist. It requires a determination that comes from knowing that the alternative is entirely unacceptable. I emphasize this requirement for perseverance in millennials who are preparing to use their voices to articulate and address pressing policy issues in innovative and new ways.

"We the people, in order to form a more perfect union, establish justice, insure domestic tranquility, provide for the common defense, promote the general welfare, and secure the blessings of liberty to ourselves and our posterity, do ordain and establish this Constitution for the United States of America."

The familiar Preamble to the United States Constitution is as powerful and pertinent today as it was in 1787. As it was authored, African Americans were enslaved by other Americans. This might sound like ancient history, but if I clearly understand that I am today a part of the "We" in the Preamble, then I can say that I possess the authority today to act on each of these statements that were written two hundred and thirty years ago. When then, I, as an African American and a woman, would not have been able to do so.

Even though I am personally too young to remember the Civil Rights Movement, I have been privy to learn that my ancestors sacrificed their blood, sweat, and tears to pave a way to a brighter future for us. I can't sit idly while their unwavering efforts are forgotten because I do not exercise my authority under the Constitution. I am not going to let the promise of the Preamble be melted from the parchment paper upon which it is written, because I don't know or understand my authority under the United States Constitution as an American citizen. I can't allow an additional obligation to diminish my ability to uphold the law of the United States, because there are forces at work that are attempting to test the validity of the laws of our nation and highest institutions. You shouldn't either, because I say so, but because you live here. You are an American citizen, and you believe in the promises of the Preamble of the Constitution and in the freedom that we have as Americans. Freedom is not free. Dr. King's life and the lives of many of our servicemen and women prove that every day. We are not perfect, but we are the greatest nation on earth. Our beliefs and rights must not be destroyed out of ignorance, fear, complacency, laziness or hypocrisy.

Let's take Dr. Martin Luther King's example and ideas to heart, and take action. Commemorating is fine, but action is better.

Published in Politic365 --

Introduction:
Believe in Yourself. Craft Your Future.

Words Have Power

CLEAR, CONCISE COMMUNICATION is the cornerstone of action. For me, the ability to communicate has been an important part of my life. Growing up, I participated in oratorical contests, and I wrote articles and essays to earn scholarship money. By the time I enrolled in college, writing had become one of my preferred methods from which to express my thoughts and disposition on a wide array of topics. I discovered that words committed to paper had the power to inspire, empower and document the greatest moments of my life. The magic of words knows no boundaries, and it gives infinite life to our observations of the world around us. Words can express the innermost sentiments of our hearts.

While at Harvard, I served on the Editorial Board of the Harvard Journal of African American Public Policy. In this role, I refined my editorial and organizational skills, and I discovered my most powerful writing voice. By the age of twenty-four, I passionately began to write a book about my life from my perspective. As the obligations of real work and real life ensued, I found myself in a methodical tango with the act of committing thoughts to paper. I would write intermittently, and then I would put it down, only to eventually pick it up again. Even so, my perspectives on social and political issues evolved, and I wrote about different experiences and perspectives gleaned from my exchanges in the world. Through studying and advancing professionally, it was safe to say I had charted new territory. With eyes wide opened, I found myself examining everything. I was commissioned to consider my role as a woman in the world while defining my stance on leadership as a productive citizen in society. The sounds of the world, good, bad and indifferent became the soundtrack for my life as well as my aspirations. I swayed to the sounds, with my pen and paper for many years, with no certainty of commitment for completion of the book that I now penned at leisure.

Life has a funny way of transforming intent into focused action. After learning of the devastating loss of my best friend, the world around me shifted. His untimely death was catastrophic for me. A loss in this manner proved to be an atmospheric shift that led me on a search for ways to honor him and his legacy. He knew that I enjoyed writing, and he also knew that I was working on a book. My best friend had been an ardent supporter, who inspired me to follow my dreams. He encouraged me to challenge the status quo. His friendship was a formidable reminder that my quest to commit words to paper and to shed light on my deepest perspectives would not be in vain. In spite of the obstacles of life, I was determined to personify the act of crafting my future.

The difficulties that we experience can result in stagnation or proactivity. I fight hard to choose proactivity every time. When we recognize how much power we have within to transform our current circumstances, we embody the fullness and resilience of whom we were destined to become. The completion of this book is resolved to serve as the establishment of another source of power from which women can feed determination. My actions and this work are dedicated to his legacy, which was the spirit of the achievement of heartfelt goals and the will to finish what we start.

A Moment in Time

In 2016, we witnessed a Presidential election with a stark contrast between a woman that some might have deemed too feminist and a misogynistic man. As a political insider, I am privy to many discussions about women in political spaces and in leadership capacities. As someone who has spent her entire existence influenced by politics, the topic of women in leadership emerges as a natural area of expertise. It is one of the areas that I know best. I have taught on American Government, the Constitution, the role of interest groups and other aspects of public policy. I have taught at the college level, and I have been a practitioner. I have worked with political candidates, trade associations and political action committees. I have knocked on doors, canvassed, advocated for legislation and policy changes, fundraised for candidates, written letters to elected officials, and even put campaign signs in people's yards. Of all the things that I have done to make an impact, I have not been a candidate, despite the suggestions and encouragement from colleagues. I believe that there are many ways to influence change. It has been my goal to experience the fullness of leadership while attaining a myriad of practical experiences from which to draw. I recognize the power of influence outside the realm of being the actual candidate. Assuming leadership in this manner has allowed me to remain focused on the things that are important to me, I have fallen into a deep romance with the practicality of leadership and politics and have committed myself accordingly.

The Framework

Leadership and politics form the thread that binds the tapestry of themes in my life. From the Civil Rights Movement to #BlackLivesMatter, #METOO, and the continuous battle for equal pay for both women and minorities, I am personally and professionally committed to the liberation of the human race in spirit and in truth. As a woman, I recognize the need for my voice to be heard and my presence to be felt. Women deserve to have a say in the laws that govern us, and in the way that decisions are made about the issues to be addressed. We must also lead the charge for action taken towards democracy and efforts to level the playing field for those who are often placed at a disadvantage. Women embody a perspective that is not always represented or present in every room where decisions are made. I challenge the notion that would have us believe that women and leadership are incongruent. I care deeply about the various factors that often hinder us from taking ownership of the many facets of our lives. We deserve to have our voices heard!

Follow the Leader is the culmination of the many lessons my experiences have taught me about life, leadership and the pursuit of happiness. I wrote this book with the fullness of my heart, and every word and sentiment is expressed to inspire and empower you to breathe life into the leader within. If by chance, the by-product of your inspiration is to take an active role in the political process at any level, the world will be better for it. No amount of involvement is too minute when we recognize our ability to impact the world around us.

A Call for the Qualified

God does not call the qualified; He qualifies the called. Whether you know it or not, you have been called to step forward in excellence. We have all been created with genius. It is up to each of us to determine the best ways to unleash the greatness that is within. In many instances, our calling is hidden amidst fear and the nuances of societal imposed standards. I have learned that neither serves as an incubator for the growth and sustainability of our dreams or the greater good of the world around us. None of these factors allows us to lead. It is in faith that we must resolve to take the necessary steps to create the world that we wish to see. Leadership is answering the call to action and taking the unprecedented ownership of all that we are destined to become.

I have spent what feels like my entire life in observance of skill sets, motivations and actions that can best be described as leadership. From our internal motivations to the goals and aspirations that result from the talent that others witness inside of each of us, I believe that we have the ability to lead in some capacity. The contents of this book are a resounding testament to that fact. The power of women and our innate ability to bring about change and centralize power to influence are more relevant now than ever. This book is meant to introduce you to a myriad of topics and perspectives from which to further develop and enhance your ideas of the concept. Just as my exposure enhanced my experiences in leadership, I wish the same for you. I wrote this book with the love and the intent that you would discover a piece of yourself and a topic or stance that will spark your internal senses and move you to take action. The pages of this book were constructed for you to dive in as you see fit. There is no one way to lead, nor is there one way to engage with this content. Every thought and every action matter, and every encounter matters.

Within the pages of this book, I share the same spirit of clarity, insight, and passion in which I have written over the past several years. It is my greatest hope that Follow the Leader will have an impact on your life, political experiences, and the way in which you think about the powerful word, "leader". It is in this same spirit of inspiration that we have the power to collectively make our country a better place.

Epigraph

"Don't discount yourself."
-Stephanie Mickle-

Table of Contents

Part I:
Leadership Unboxed

"Leadership is multifaceted and must be examined from a variety of perspectives."

-Stephanie Mickle-

Introduction

WHAT CAN BE said of names such as Nelson Mandela and Barack Obama? They stand alone in merit and in truth for what they represent in our country. They represent hope, pride and nationalism for people of color, the oppressed, forgotten, misled, misinformed or those in need of a hero.

Under their leadership, our world has been fortunate to feel optimistic that good things would happen, even in the face of degradation, destruction, and attack. To be a citizen under leaders who demonstrate a genuine concern for the human race is among our greatest gifts. For me, their examples are what leadership at its best looks like. Figures, who authentically connect with humanity, can change a paradigm and call people to a higher level of themselves. Leadership in this capacity is the way in which we stand united and step forward in unison.

Nelson Mandela was able to shepherd his people and ultimately a nation through the end of apartheid and into a new democracy. President Obama ushered in a period where hopefulness abounded for the prospect of racial reconciliation and progress. He did not make the United States a perfect union -- nor did he attempt to -- but he moved us towards a more perfect union. The hearts and minds of people were changed because of President Obama's presence as the leader of the free world and a two-term president who won both the popular and electoral vote. Many people began to understand that global leadership is a quality of humanity. Bearing witness to the election that changed

3

the fate of the ability to hope for people of all races, creeds, and colors was among my greatest lessons in leadership.

Early on the morning of November 4, 2008, I was in Cape Town, South Africa watching the United States Presidential elections at the home of the Consul General, along with two hundred other people, mostly Americans and South Africans. I had attended an election returns party at the home of the United States' Consul General in South Africa along with two hundred other Americans and expatriates from around the world. Wireless laptops were set up on one side of the Consul General's home for those people wanting to check on the status of any state or local race. An inviting breakfast buffet was prepared on the other side of the house. Television monitors were scattered about the home and outside on the terrace. Due to the time difference, it was an early morning in Cape Town, and the atmosphere was filled with jubilation and a certain anticipation. Having watched many election returns stateside, I quickly found that nothing could quite compare to watching a United States Presidential election through an international lens. Though the event itself was not partisan, most of the people who had come that morning to watch the elections were Obama supporters. When it was finally announced that Barack Obama had won the election and was to become the 44th President of the United States of America, all of the various news accounts about Barack Obama, the person, and the discussions of the potential impact of a change in U.S. foreign policy once again were engulfed by the beauty of the mountain view from the terrace and the quiet of the South African morning.

A week earlier, upon arriving in Cape Town for the holiday, my friends and I encountered a similar scenario. As we visited different places and people learned that we were American, they immediately asked the following two questions: "Did you vote before you left to come to South Africa?" and "For whom did you vote?" The answers to these questions were of utmost importance to the people we encountered. We were in a country still fresh with the memory of independence and the right to vote for all South Africans. Nelson Mandela its first Black President, had been elected only fourteen years earlier. While we had come to enjoy the beauty of South Africa, it became quickly apparent wherever we went that the nation of South Africa was just as beautiful as it was politically astute. I was first asked these questions by the gentleman in customs who reviewed my United States passport. I was startled to be asked these questions immediately following my eighteen-hour flight to Cape Town. For a moment, I wondered if I might be sent back to the United States if I failed to correctly answer the questions from enquirers. Fortunately, I was prepared to answer correctly by the time the questions were posed days later by dinner companions and locals who were eagerly following the Presidential elections in the United States.

While in Cape Town, I also had the opportunity to visit Robben Island, the now-defunct jail where Nelson Mandela spent twenty-seven years in prison after being convicted for his political activities and challenges to the Apartheid regime. Seeing the cold, hard, tiny cell where he had been held made me ponder what it must have taken for him to have survived there for a life sentence. Nelson Mandela was so full of life and hope after having been sentenced to such a stark existence. That life sentence was interrupted by the fall of the South African Apartheid regime. My greatest gift, from having these experiences, resulted in my gaining extensive insight and the understanding of the use of concepts and laurels in leadership. It is upon these principles that we hold the power to harness the essence of thought, innovation, and freedom. This power enables us to move into action to craft the present and the future.

i. Theories of Leadership, Women's Styles of Leadership, Formal vs. Informal, Inherent vs. Expressive

The leadership styles of women can be traced as far back as our humanity. There is notable evidence to prove that women exerted leadership during every era of our existence. Today, the concept of women and leadership is what some may recognize as a trending topic. While this trend continues to rise in popularity, it has always been the undercurrent of the greatest moments in our history. Whether the world has deemed it necessary to see the value in the leadership of women or not, the world as we know it cannot exist in the absence of the tutelage and guiding hands of women.

In the Beginning

The prolific story of Adam and Eve provides us with a poignant example of the continuum of the relationship between leadership and influence. Adam was given instruction by God to take care of the Garden of Eden. He was charged with a position of power. God gave Adam a helpmate in Eve to ensure that he would be fully equipped to carry out his assigned tasks. As the story unfolds, Eve meets with the serpent, who introduces her to the forbidden fruit. As a result of the meeting, Eve shares her desire to eat of the fruit. It was at that moment that the lines between leadership and influence intertwined. It can be argued that Eve's ability to coerce Adam to eat of the fruit was an act of leadership. Others might counter that Eve used influence, and Adam deemed that the leader was responsible for the final decision.

If asked, I would have to say that Eve's contribution was that of an influential decision maker. If leadership is determined to be executed by those who make the decisions, Adam would be accountable for the final say. In both scenarios presented, there are opportunities for influence. The most glaring factor is that the concept of leadership and influence is interrelated. I challenge the notion that one can exist in the absence of the other. With history as the backdrop, we continue to see more examples of the multifaceted relationship between leadership and influence.

It is imperative for women to recognize the historical patterns of leadership that have helped to shape the display that we see today. Understanding the methods of leadership is just as crucial as the ability to lead. There are times when we have seen ourselves in the historical context of the ideologies of leadership; however, we have been effective in adapting models to best suit our pursuit of goals or to arrive at an intended destination. The following women leaders crafted their personal leadership styles: Joan of Arc displayed a militant style of leadership. Madeleine Albright's leadership style could be classified as business oriented, and Ellen Johnson Sirleaf, President of Liberia, established a framework for diplomacy. Mother Teresa personified leadership through peace. Women have assumed leadership positions and implemented new and innovative models from which to navigate the needs of the world. Accordingly, women have demonstrated that there is not one unique way to lead. Leadership is vast, and it encompasses the associated sets that are utilized for efficacy and success. A closer look at leadership and diplomacy, through the countless examples given to us over the years, further proves that the lines between leadership and influence merge to create an equation for world change.

Forward Fashion. Forward March.

Most women love fashion, not necessarily high fashion as runway models, but dressing and choosing our most flattering colors. Many women love to adorn themselves in jewelry, outfits, shoes, and sometimes even hats. As a little girl, I often played dress up in my mother's closet as I dreamed of being the belle of the ball like Cinderella in my favorite Disney stories. Fashion can also be a representation of one's leadership style. For example, Madeleine Albright, former U.S. Secretary of State is by definition a leader. I once read a book about her subtle, yet powerful leadership style. She was known to have worn different brooches as she attended diplomatic meetings. Each brooch was carefully selected as it represented her political intention and posture for the meeting. This ethereal strategy of nonverbal communication indicated whether she was coming to engage in civil discourse or by way of force. Everyone always wondered what she would be wearing, and it became a significant point of interest. Many women are criticized for certain fashion choices, but Madeline Albright transformed the meaning of her brooches into a way to communicate and to lead in foreign policy and diplomacy.

Queen Elizabeth by definition is a leader. She is the head of the British Monarchy. She is not the Prime Minister, and she is not seen debating for laws on the floor of Parliament or belting out demands. It is possible that people may not see her as a traditional leader from such based upon outward appearances alone, but she is still the Queen.

Accordingly, she gives us another standard of leadership that is neither aggressive or verbal. Her style of dress and her demeanor further exemplify the fact that women lead in innovative ways not traditionally recognized as leadership. It should be noted that these methods still prove to be effective.

As a petite figure, Queen Elizabeth recognized early in her reign that she could not easily be seen in a crowd due to her height. As a leader, visibility is key. With careful thought and strategy, her presence was and is still today made apparent through her ritual of wearing bright clothing.

Hillary Clinton has a stellar resume and a history of leadership exploits in the more traditional sense. She could also be categorized as using attire to communicate her disposition in politics and diplomacy. She is a known lover of pantsuits and changing hairstyles. Often, she has received a great deal of backlash about her pantsuits, largely because naysayers felt that they were not feminine enough, and neither was she. Critiques stated that she was manly and not feminine enough. Her supporters, many of them women, believed that her leadership style, message, and example of women being empowered were just the opposite. Hillary Clinton demonstrated, that it is possible for a woman to wear a pantsuit and make a resounding fashion statement that says, "although I am a woman, I am capable of leading just as effectively as a man."

Michelle Obama personified physical fitness, and her fitness initiatives were appealing to children. Her zeal for engaging children in learning healthy eating lifestyles caught the attention of America. She will always be remembered for inviting children to the White House garden to taste freshly grown vegetables. We had not seen a First Lady of the United States wearing workout clothes and doing exercises before Michelle Obama. She was revered and criticized for her sculpted arms, but she bared them proudly as she wore sleeveless dresses and ball gowns. Her leadership and influence led the world to honor women who are physically fit. We celebrate her efforts to encourage a healthy lifestyle for women and children. Michelle Obama was also a fashion trendsetter, and the world took note of her choices in ensembles. The conversation on first ladies and fashion could not be held in the absence of the great Jacqueline Kennedy Onassis, who remains an iconic figure for what she chose to wear and her representation of style and grace. In this same light, it must also be mentioned that Princess Diana by definition was a leader. She was fashionable, and she used her influence to bring attention to the humanitarian issues that were important to her. Her efforts in addressing the needs of children in impoverished countries will always be recognized.

Interestingly enough, there is not a lot of discussion surrounding what men wear. Women have often had to contend with criticism and critiques, but they have used it as a way to lead and demonstrate progress. I encourage women to embrace fashion as a way to expand influence and leadership. It has been done by these women on the world stage. I believe that many others will use this powerful strategy to embrace the work that is before us.

As much as women would like to avoid the great debate regarding appearance and perception, these ladies' examples are proof that books are indeed judged by their covers. When used as a strategy for leadership, this sentiment is not necessarily a bad notion to conceive.

Leveraging Influence

Leadership, which constitutes a less formal act of guidance, can be classified as formal or implied. Formal leadership denotes that a person has the title, their name is on the door, and they sign the papers. If we study history, we would glean that women received the opportunity to formally lead much later than men.

Some might argue that women's leadership is more concentric in nature. We have always been energetic in assembling our friends, husbands, cousins, and neighbors, but we have not tackled world issues with the same zeal. We are excellent leaders by virtue of collaborations. These models of leadership are trusted means to a desired end, and they can be effectively used to benefit and impact a large audience. Women's involvement in the political process is a gateway for a myriad of leadership styles. Women must be included in the conversations and processes that lead to generational changes.

Many women throughout history, who did not have an officially expressed title in government, had the tremendous ability to influence. Cleopatra influenced Mark Antony. The Queen of Sheba influenced Solomon. Nancy Reagan influenced Ronald Reagan. These women were leaders in their own right, and through their influence, they amplified their leadership skills and that of the men to whom they were connected.

We can point to many examples in history where women have been influential in their ability to lead. Leadership skills, even in patriarchal societies where women did not have many rights, have been effectively implored. Today, you may see a male who signifies a leader who is getting ready to make a decision to vote "yes" on a certain initiative. After speaking with a mother, daughter, wife, girlfriend or sister, his opinion might change. Opinions, data and the sentiments of others can be influential in decision making. Grandmothers reading this book especially know this to be true. Who does not love to go to Grandma's house to see what she has baked? Grandma knows that if she needs to talk to her grandson about his progress in school, she can make him a sandwich or bake cookies and sit down with him. Personal time with her grandson can lead to a life-changing experience. This is an informal construct of leadership. Informal constructs demonstrate that there is power to influence the decisions that will be made.

This same influence exists in the maternal realm. The power of maternal leadership is indeed an informal force. Women have inherently been given influence using this method. It is not an uncommon practice to hear a man speak of what his mother has requested of him in a given scenario. Some of the most powerful men have been known to yield to the direction of their mothers, and they embrace and celebrate their influence.

Another example of women's leadership that has had powerful effects on society is Mothers Against Drunk Driving (MADD). MADD has evolved as a nationally recognized organization that was established by a mother who mobilized scores of supporters. She created a movement because someone had enacted a heinous act against her child. This organization is now a recognized entity in the political process. Their voices are not silenced, and the nation is better for it.

Lastly, Oprah Winfrey is a classic example of the power of a woman's influence in leadership. If she endorses a product or makes a statement, the public opinion is subject to be influenced. There is great power in influence. To further demonstrate the implications of influence, there was even great chatter of Oprah running for president. Many felt that she had the ability to lead the country in a positive direction. Over the years, her career in media has proven to be one of the most powerful and influential of our time, and it portrays a demonstration of the synergy that women's leadership can create.

Outside of the Box

It is tempting to place leadership in a box; however, we discover the greatest sources of power, just outside the box. The exercise of leadership can occur at a granular level just as effectively as it can amidst the widely known formal practices.

Traditionally, we have been acculturated to recognize leadership only when demonstrated in a forward or aggressive context. Everyone does not define leadership in the same way. An open mind allows us to access a myriad of viewpoints and arrive at our own destination regarding best practices and the exercise of methods to lead and influence.

Theoretically defining and dissecting leadership can be critical skills in the understanding of a concept and in determining how we exercise our power on a daily basis. We are called to recognize the impact of leadership and its influence on our lives, in our communities, and in the world at large. Careful examination of the concept of leadership leads us to conclude that leadership is inherently, actually, and structurally intertwined.

As women, we have been thrust into opportunities to utilize each of those skills. We can be more impactful when we advance our understanding of leadership skills by becoming more actively involved in the process. The better we understand them, the more effective and impactful we can be. We are not limited to one model of influence or one mode of leadership. If a woman understands her inherent power, and her ability to exercise influence, then she can become a very effective leader, in a formal or informal position. In this space, a woman has the authority to capitalize on leadership models that are unassuming, yet powerful.

In my city, my specialty might be baking oatmeal raisin cookies. If I send those cookies to individuals that I want to influence or with whom I need to establish a business connection, and they like oatmeal raisin cookies— then I have just established a relationship that can prove to be beneficial for those with whom I share similar interests. Exercising influence can lead to unspoken connections that can be profitable for those who do business around me. If someone connected to me, like a friend or family member, then wants to do business with someone with whom I have sent oatmeal raisin cookies, a relationship lead has already been generated upon which they can build.

This same train of thought can translate to leadership in community-related endeavors. There are so many ways to be influential. If I see a need at my child's school, I can step into a position of service to influence positive change and forward progression. An example of this would be serving as the leader of the Parent Teachers Association (PTA). Accordingly, action in this manner converts well into the political process.

Right now, there is someone in the United States Congress or Senate receiving lemon bars, banana bread or baked goods of some sort from someone in the district. No one refuses items such as these because they are delicious. The value of this gesture is also below the gift ban, which means that the delicacies are fair game to be enjoyed. Receiving items such as these establishes a deeper connection to the community for both the giver and the receiver. Any gift this simple communicates "you matter". It is the simplest form of relationship development. Relationships are built on this type of give and take and result in the establishment of a longstanding history. Many women do this well because we are relationally driven. We love to talk to our girlfriends, connect with loved ones, spend time with family and give generously. We are naturally gifted to do this. Do all women cultivate it? I would venture to say that the answer is "no", but many do.

I challenge you to ask yourself the following questions:

What are my best gifts? How can I use these same gifts to influence the community at large and the political process? How can I leverage these gifts to become a leader?

Formal leadership in politics is winning an election, receiving a political appointment or an official title. Examples of informal leadership are networking, lobbying, and coalition building. Both methodologies are important and are necessary for moving the needle for change. Much of what I speak of is comprised of action and the complexities of the power to influence and get things done in the political world.

Accountability in leadership cannot be optional. If we empower leadership in the absence of accountability, we establish a path for failed outcomes. Consider the leader whose company gets in trouble for a decision that is made. Some leaders may believe that the buck stops with them or that if it happened on their watch, then they must assume responsibility. Some leaders may place blame on staff members or a rogue employee. To me, accountability is a question of leadership. A leader, or one desiring to be in a position to lead, must always ask herself a series of questions when things go well and when moments for development arise. The most significant considerations are accountability and prevention of unwanted outcomes. One conclusion that is drawn by an accountable leader is whether more substantive training could have been provided and received.

Even amidst the resolve of accountability, there is the presence of leadership. Leadership is not reflected in instances where the person in charge determines only to place blame or to pretend to be oblivious to the series of events that transpire. In leadership, everyone is accountable. It is not leadership to only blame others when you are in charge.

Starbucks invited a firestorm after one of their employees called the police on two guests who were waiting for a business contact to arrive. The men, unarmed, non-violent and posing no threat to the store, were senselessly arrested and escorted out of the venue. The scenario was escalated as the Starbucks employee was white and the entrepreneurs were two men of color. The then Starbucks, Chairman, stood before the public and took full responsibility for the series of events as they had unfolded. Taking a clear leadership stance and being accountable for the acts of an employee were effective diversion strategies that prevented what could have been a huge economic failure for Starbucks. He acknowledged that this situation happened on his watch, and he resolved to apologize until people believed him, and trust was restored. The result was more focused on his leadership than on the rogue employee; therefore, the public's attention was shifted towards the Chairman's ability to lead the company out of crisis.

When we refer back to the story of Adam and Eve, some believe that Eve was at fault because she disobeyed God and that Adam showed a lack of leadership by blaming her. Leadership is not about placing blame; it is about taking responsibility. It is imperative to understand that effective leadership always embraces a level of integrity. Another approach within the realm of leadership could be for Adam to declare that it was Eve's fault. Adam could have recommended that Eve is fired, voted out of office, or replaced. In this scenario, were God to agree and ultimately make such a decision, it would still be an act of leadership that assumes responsibility for the changes and adaptations to a plan that can be made to bring about a different set of results.

ii. Philosophies of Leadership

We all have developed our own philosophies and viewpoints around what a leader is and what a leader looks like. My philosophy of leadership has evolved over time. I have always seen myself as a leader in some capacity because I have always maintained a vision for the things that I would like to see happen in the world around me. In high school, I was the president of various clubs or the vice president of various organizations. I was number one on my line when I pledged for my sorority. Even though there were three of us who were the same height, I chose to be number one. My leadership style has always been innate, but my approaches have changed over time.

You can be an authoritarian, a collaborator, or somewhere in between. You can be someone who motivates by demand or through encouragement. Even though my sense of vision has been clear, I have learned throughout my career how to better empower my team or those around me. I have since understood the importance and effectiveness of being a better delegator. There is massive power to be discovered in the act of giving people room to execute amidst their own strengths and in their talents. I subscribe to the notion that the best leaders are those who can also follow. Understanding when it is time to be in charge to run the meeting or to allow someone on the team to do so is the ultimate display of leadership. Leadership is recognizing that there is a place for executive decision making and also for training and development. The most effective leaders are those who build their teams to empower each member to be more successful and to be the best representation of the leader. I profess that this is where I am in my space now.

I can recall being a member at Macedonia Missionary Baptist Church in Orlando, Florida. As a member, I belonged to the Social Service Ministry. Our tasks included stocking the food pantry and the clothes closet. It was not a glamorous ministry, yet our efforts were rooted in service to others. Sorting the clothes and counting the cans were tasks performed behind the scenes, but the quality of our work was what was most important. I fell in love with the opportunity to serve with integrity in this capacity, and I learned the power in leading from the rear.

When you believe yourself to be a good person, you can assume responsibility for a position that allows you to use your gifts and talents in the absence of praise, while building humility and activating gratitude.

The role of a servant leader reinforced my ideal and understanding of the marriage of service and leadership and further proved that they can and should happen at the same time. This is what Jesus did as He washed his disciples' feet and taught them about what they needed to know to be successful. He empowered people to have hope for a better way to live. He modeled servant leadership and the acceptance that we can be comfortable in our ability to know and perform whatever tasks are before us. Former President Barack Obama was the leader of the free world, but he never had a problem holding his own umbrella. He was a prominent example of a leader who demonstrated respect for humanity. It is my belief that the highest calling is being able to both serve and lead. Even if society would have us to believe that leadership is rooted in oversight of demands, people respect those who adhere to the rules of engagement that call leaders to serve in good faith. The demonstration of respect at a human level allows us to connect in ways that are unimaginable. Leadership through service is both impactful and inspirational. This style of leadership attracts those who wish to follow a charge for change based on humanity, and it constitutes a win for all parties involved.

Fearless Leadership

I have to laugh at the amount of times that I have made a decision to do something that many have questioned if and when it would work. I have been labeled fearless by many of my colleagues. This descriptor is reflective of my philosophies on leadership. By the time I have made the decision, I have managed to work through whatever fear and/or reservations that I might have had in a given scenario. There is an assuredness in decision making that allows each of us to operate in the absence of fear.

People would ask me questions like, "Why did you go so far from home for college?" "Did you have any concerns about going to Harvard?" None of these scenarios caused me any concern. I have always recognized that fear cannot be the reason to ignore great opportunities.

Fearless leadership requires that decisions be made using an internal compass. Rather than committing time to conceptualize what can go wrong in a scenario, I choose to find ways to make the decision work. I often encourage my staff to find a way to win. I have, however, discovered that the exceptions for going after every great opportunity will surface in my consideration of the people that I love.

In some cases, I have turned down great opportunities if I felt that a loved one needed me more. I had to grow to get to a level of comfort to know that someone was okay, and I needed to get back to pursuing my dreams. I had to recognize that loved ones would find a place of understanding, and their understanding would relieve me of such hesitation.

Leadership Footprint

With skill sets as vast as the faces of the people that fill the world, I am reminded on a continual basis that we are all present to lead and thrive in different capacities. We are not meant to exercise leadership in the same way. The less we embrace the differences, the more productive we will be in solving the greatest problems in our nation.

I have coined the term "leadership footprint" as the embodiment of the consciousness that I believe we should all seek regarding the impact that we can and should have in the world in which we live. If we identify and categorize our actions on a daily basis and sort through those actions to determine our areas of greatest success, we will be led towards the very thing that we can do to help others. This same leadership footprint can also be referred to as purpose. So many spend so much time in search of purpose, but I believe that our purpose is just beneath the surface of the day to day life that creates so much noise that often distracts us.

Most people possess a desire to be heard, acknowledged and recognized for their leadership footprint. As such, there is much value in the development and use of formal skill sets for leadership that can be learned by anyone, even though the individual leadership footprint is case specific. We all possess an ability to lead. The greater question that arises is, what then will we do with our ability to lead?

Deep Roots

"If one generation plants a field of seeds, another generation is blessed to eat of its fruit."

-Stephanie Mickle-

Family History

My family history is deeply rooted in the efficacy of love, hard work, education, generosity, legacy, and excellence. I grew up with a large, close-knit, extended family of aunts, uncles, grandparents, parents, godparents and my neighborhood parents. I was reared by a village, and I am the better for it.

My great-grandmother was a chambermaid for a wealthy white woman. My great-grandfather was a minister, and they worked hard to give both of their sons, one being my grandfather, the best life possible. It was because of her work that she and my great-grandfather could afford to send my grandfather, Andrew Richardson Mickle, to a private school called Mather Academy, which was located in Camden, South Carolina. He would establish his educational roots as a day student at the premier boarding school that became home and an educational breeding ground for wealthy, African American students. In his home and at his school, he witnessed the lasting and persistent effects of diligence, and he adopted these behaviors as his own. During this time, he became skilled in the craft of tailoring and found it to be a lucrative way to express himself. He was also an active member of the football team and adopted what would develop as a continuous ritual for a healthy lifestyle.

At the conclusion of high school, my grandfather moved to Columbia, South Carolina. It was there that he met my grandmother, Grace. She was beautiful and had a fun, playful spirit according to my grandfather. They dated for a spell and got married. Shortly after their union, my grandfather was drafted to go to Paris to fight in World War II. He also spent time in France. Before his departure, my father was conceived. While pregnant, and in an attempt to be closer to family while my grandfather was at war, my grandmother moved to New York City. My grandmother, Grace, welcomed my father into the world while my grandfather was still away on assignment in the Army.

After the war ended, my grandfather returned. During that era, there was an ordered period of decompression for veterans. The policy in the military was that veterans needed dedicated time and space to transition and re-acclimate back into normal life or life as they had known it before their deployment. After that period ended, my grandfather decided to complete his college education on the GI Bill at a relatively new school located in Daytona, Florida, founded by Mary McLeod Bethune. Upon enrolling into Bethune Cookman College, he took his wife and son, my father, to begin a new life in Florida. My grandmother, Grace, had a degree in business, and she became the personal secretary for Mrs. Bethune. She was tasked with personally attending to the affairs of Mrs. Bethune. I am told that my father, who was a toddler at the time, spent time playing at Mrs. Bethune's office. During those years, they also welcomed their second son, Andrew.

To say that my grandparents were progressive would be an understatement. My grandmother had a professional career in the 1940s and 1950s, and my grandfather was both an entrepreneur with a tailoring and alterations business in Daytona with his friend, Bob Wright, and an extremely active college student. While studying mathematics, he also became a member of the swim team and played tennis in college. He had adopted a healthy lifestyle and very much favored being physically fit and active, since his days of playing football in high school. Together, they worked hand in hand to create a life for themselves and their two children. Amidst the hustle and bustle of life, the onset of marital problems ensued.

Back in the 1950's, couples did not typically separate, but my grandmother returned to New York City to be with her family, and my grandfather remained in Daytona Beach. There was a great deal of mystery and speculation surrounding her departure. Many wondered why she had not taken the children with her?

The passing of a full year apart would prompt my grandfather to make the decision to legally file for a divorce. The grounds for divorce cited were abandonment. As a result of his filing, the court awarded him custody of both my father and his brother, my uncle. After the proceedings, my grandmother resurfaced. It was then that my grandfather made the decision to send his young sons, my dad, and my uncle to South Carolina to live with their grandparents. My grandfather was determined to take some time to get his life together and recenter himself. For three years following the divorce, my father and his younger brother lived with my great-grandparents in South Carolina.

My grandmother, Grace, would come to see them for court-appointed supervised visits. As the months passed, the visits eventually stopped. My father nor my uncle would see her again until her funeral some years later when they were young men. This also meant that my siblings nor I would be afforded the opportunity to meet her.

A Ribbon in the Sky

Three years later, my grandfather met and became enamored with a lady named Catherine. He both admired and pursued her. Catherine was a co-ed student enrolled at Bethune Cookman College on a music scholarship. She was very beautiful. Initially, she expressed to my grandfather that she had an interest in becoming Miss Bethune Cookman College and that the prospect of a man with a family did not align with her campus goals. He continued to demonstrate his interest in her and even went as far as to design and sew custom-made outfits and gowns with matching earrings for her pageants in his tailoring business. At

25

the age of twenty-one, Catherine would become his second wife and the figure that my siblings and I would come to know, love and revere as our grandmother.

The day after uniting in holy matrimony, the happy couple immediately went to South Carolina to get my father and my uncle to bring them back to Florida to begin their new life together as a blended family. Together, they would raise the two boys as well as give birth to two more sons. Throughout the years, Grandma Catherine never made a distinction between any of her children, blended or biological. After all, Grandma Catherine had married a man with two children who had recently experienced a painful divorce. She had been a product of a separation and divorce, and she knew what it felt like for her parents to split up and be reared by a stepparent. My grandparents continued to work collaboratively to construct the lives they willed while raising four college educated successful men and cultivating stability and a blueprint for the family module that my siblings and I would eventually experience.

In retrospect, I give my Grandma Catherine a great deal of credit for her bravery. She entered into a marriage that encompassed so many elements of uncertainty, and she did so with class and dignity. She has been a rock for our family and is due to a tremendous amount of praise for setting an exemplary standard of class. She was and still is the embodiment of a southern belle.

Grandma Catherine worked for many years as an educator, with a mission to ensure that she was impactful in her efforts to empower students with practical business skills that would make them viable forces in the workforce. Her love for her students and people in general spilled over into her presence in the community.

In addition, as a recognized socialite, there was no limit to Grandma's involvement in the community at large. From engagement through a tremendous amount of volunteer work, to singing in the choir, founding the Saturday Academy at Mt. Carmel Baptist Church, serving as a member of the deaconess board, and a member of The Links, Inc., The Visionaires and her beloved sorority, Alpha Kappa Alpha Sorority, Inc., she has never missed a beat.

"Daddy Mick"

My grandfather affectionately referred to as "Daddy Mick" by all who loved him was what I would describe as a force of nature. He was just as social as my grandmother. There was no limit to his impact and his involvement. His activities included: the Boys and Girls Club, The Board of the Gardenia Gardens Project (a public housing project), serving as a Deacon in his church, Alpha Phi Alpha Fraternity, Inc., and the Bethune Cookman College Alumni Association. Both my grandmother and grandfather loved attending football games and fundraising for their beloved alma mater.

They were school teachers by day and entrepreneurial trendsetters by night; innovation was in their blood. He ran a tailoring business out of the home while my grandmother ran a typing business out of the home. My grandfather also taught private swimming lessons. As God saw fit, my grandfather became the community swimming instructor and is credited today with teaching thousands of African American children to swim. He was eventually honored by the designating of a new municipal swimming pool owned by the City of Gainesville, Florida in his namesake, the Andrew R. Mickle Municipal Pool.

Family Ties

My parents, Stephan and Evelyn, met and married while in college. They were two of the first African Americans to integrate the University of Florida in the 1960s during the very tumultuous times of the Civil Rights Movement. That experience of desegregation forged a bond that few who have not had a similar experience can truly understand. My mother, Evelyn, was the first African American to integrate the College of Nursing and matriculate and is a Registered Nurse. My father, Stephan, is a retired Federal Judge, and he was the first African American undergraduate to matriculate from the University of Florida. In addition to their respective professional accomplishments, they are generous with their time, wisdom and resources. Excellence is a precedent that can never be erased from the fibers of our DNA, and my parents' experiences were another testament to its value.

We grew up going to church every Sunday, and afterward having Sunday dinner where we discussed the activities for the week, homework assignments, current events and other family commitments that were on the schedule. My mother was a Sunday School teacher, and my father served on the Trustee Board of the church. Both of my parents were very active on community boards and in organizations. My father enjoyed mentoring young African American males who had gotten in trouble with the system. My mom liked to work with children and youth at church and in the Women's Ministry. Our family spent time every summer at Crescent Beach near St. Augustine, Florida. We loved cooking out, playing in the pool and in the ocean for hours. We had so much fun making pizza and watching movies. We would invite our childhood friends, and my father would teach my brother to fish and play "shark games" with all of us in the pool. When I was ready to go off to college, my parents wore their college sweatshirts proudly and often visited me on the ivy-clad campuses of Smith College and Harvard University.

No matter what was happening around us, it was always clear that family was first. If my father needed to travel for his work, most times my mother traveled with him. If someone had to work late, my parents could count on my grandparents, aunts, uncles or neighborhood parents to ensure our care. During the summertime, when both my grandparents and parents were working, no stone was left unturned. Everyone pitched in to keep our family on track, and we all learned to support one another. If someone had something going on, whether it be a recital or a speaking engagement, sporting contest or what have you, the Mickles were going to show up and show our support for one another.

My grandparents also frequently picked up my siblings, Amy, Stephan II and me from school. Both my father and mother had careers that required their attention, and my siblings and I spent many afternoons at my grandparents' house, which we loved. To see Daddy Mick coming was always a treat. He kept a huge smile on his face, and we were so excited to see him. We learned that on any given day, he would always have the same three things in his pocket. He would have his keys, his money, and his breath mints. As kids, we delighted in knowing that we were going to either go for a ride, get some money from him or get some potato chips and a soda. On a special day, we might just get all three. His generosity knew no limits where his grandchildren were concerned.

Grandma Catherine always had a fresh pound cake in the kitchen, and she made the best sweet tea. Her pantry was never empty. On any given day, you could discover bustling conversations and laughter coming from my grandparents' home. Everyone, ranging from the neighborhood kids to friends who just randomly stopped by, filled the home with conversation, love, and laughter. My grandfather was a father to many of the fatherless children in the community, especially young men. The swimming pool in my grandparents' backyard and pool table in their home served as the backdrop for fun. My grandparents had the ability to make everyone feel welcomed. The doors of their home were always opened to guests, and their home was always filled with people and pets. It seemed as though there was always room for one more pet in their house. My uncle, Darryl, who later became a veterinarian, was often responsible for the welcoming of new pets, and my Uncle Jeff, my dad's youngest brother, was like a big brother to my siblings and me. As kids, we loved our visits with our uncle Drew and aunt Yolanda, and the ever opened doors and arms of my aunt, Veronica, who lived next door to us.

No price tag can be placed on the value of family closeness, support and working together. We were taught to look for ways to show our love throughout the year. Christmas was unique in that we exchanged gifts by pulling names. It was a form of Secret Santa, and we loved making it a game. We pulled names at Thanksgiving and then on Christmas Day, we revealed the names and gifts. Many traditions established the foundation for our family, and they are still ever present today.

Daddy Mick was hardworking, intelligent, responsible, compassionate, and a wonderful provider; he lived life with zest and a smile. He personified strength and was without question the strong patriarch of our family. He earned our love and respect, and we were happy to spend time with him. Beyond the warm beautiful smile, he did not play. He was protective of our whole family. We all knew who was in charge, and no one had a problem with it. He was a producer of love, respect, resources, and he was everything that we needed in a father figure.

Because of our family interactions, my siblings, cousins and I were privileged to witness my grandparents interact as adult parents to my father and his three brothers. Many of the same core values they taught us were instilled in my father and uncles first. Instilled in all four of their sons were generosity, Christian foundations, and good moral character. Likewise, hard work and discipline were paramount. They all learned how to do what we referred to as "manly" things, like changing a tire and fixing things around the house. Working together, they could fix everything, it seemed.

Daddy Mick was also not shy in expressing how much he loved my grandmother. Grandma Catherine was a beauty queen at Stanton High School in Jacksonville, Florida, and I remember that I had the opportunity to attend a high school reunion where someone was proudly showing off a swimsuit photo of my grandmother in the high school yearbook. My grandfather was furious! I could not help but smile and marvel that after forty years of marriage he still would get jealous when other men looked at his wife. When my grandparents were ready to celebrate fifty years of marriage, our family had a grand celebration in their honor. After everyone had finished honoring the happy couple, my grandmother made it a point to tell every ear that could hear: "*I just want you all to know that we are in love.*" It was such a remarkable testament to a real-life love story. Over the years, they have shared with me that they have had problems, like any other relationship, but their commitment sustained them to withstand the test of time. They were married for fifty-seven years before my grandfather passed.

My family's presence in my life has helped me to never see excellence as optional. Their words and actions have deeply instilled love, courage, perseverance, and innovation inside my soul.

Political Things

When I was a child, children were expected to be seen and not heard when adults were talking. My grandfather had a number of friends who were involved in local politics, and I had access to many of their conversations from which to learn and gain perspective. I remember talks about what meetings needed to be held and who needed to be there, as well as what types of issues were essential to those present at the meetings. I can clearly recall those conversations and now recognize them as strategy sessions. These intimate conversations became the backdrop of my political roots.

My grandfather, who often led the charge during the meetings, spoke with authority. He was always confident but respectful of everyone. His communication style was clear and orderly. He had a gift in his ability to articulate what he was looking for from a candidate who wanted his blessing. He was a valued voice and presence in the community and a leader who could help a candidate get votes from the other African Americans in the community. He would listen, and after hearing all of the facts, he would tell the person, "Now, I have heard you out." I could always tell that he was listening by his body language and demeanor. He would not always commit to a decision to support a candidate on the spot. It became apparent to me over the years that he would ponder choices of this magnitude of importance. Upon ending most conversations, he would say that he would be in touch. I admired his approach to politics and the fact that he recognized the impact of his actions for not just our family but the community at large. Watching him allowed me to witness a power broker in the political process. Serving in this capacity also meant that he was often solicited by many requesting his support. He did not take this role lightly because there were unspoken rules of engagement, and my grandfather was a key player.

One particular meeting that I can recall attending was held in a bustling room filled with influencers discussing, planning and constructing a list of actions and assigning roles as to who would be responsible for carrying them out. The common goal that they were working towards was an execution of support to see someone that they supported is nominated or appointed. The meeting revealed the conversations that needed to be had, money that needed to be raised and how to garner support for the candidate of choice. This meeting, among many others, reinforced the need for strategy, much like what my grandfather had mapped out. Being present also provided me with impactful insight as to the need for action-oriented goals to yield desired results. I also gleaned that there was not one set role. Everyone in the room had a viable way from which to contribute, and he or she were all necessary to win.

In that meeting, questions came up such as: Whom, are you going to put your energy and resources behind? How does a candidate craft a plan of action to do so in a way that doesn't offend others? Success in this regard is no easy feat. There are many factors to consider when determining a candidate to support. Could it be based on timing, seniority or competence? Should decisions be based on a demonstrated track record of leadership? Alternatively, should the one who can have the most significant impact be the candidate of choice? I would venture to say that my grandfather listened for all of these things and made assessments accordingly. In the end, he always made a decision and stood firmly behind it. His demonstration of commitment to the political process introduced me to a skillful position of power that was not seen by the public. The relevance of this approach to politics is the cornerstone of my belief that every person can be impactful if there is the recognition of the skill set that can be contributed to the process and activate people from where they stand. My grandfather taught me that the political process is not a one size fits all arena; however, it is the execution of a solid strategy that can bring about significant change in a community.

Excellence Has No Color

If by chance, we aspire to excellence, and the accrual of legacy, we must also assume responsibility for the associated costs. By watching the leaders of my family, I learned at a very early age that one price of legacy is freedom. The continued establishment of heritage has been paramount for my family. In that quest to build a legacy that withstands the test of time and one that establishes an inheritance of excellence, we were taught that sometimes you have to grin and bear it. My father never allowed us to forget the fact that there would be times in our lives that things would not appear to be fair. Watching him maneuver professionally was the ultimate demonstration of leadership. He used all of who and what he was to create a sustainable life for our family and those who will come after him.

My siblings and I were witnesses to the fact that walking in excellence also meant that there would be times that you had to do things to stay in a position. That could mean having a presence at functions that you would rather not attend, conversing with people that you'd rather not converse, or withholding your most exact sentiments to refrain from negative publicity. As a prominent family of color, we recognized that these things were no different than what white families, with political ties, experienced. The significant difference, from our perspective, is that the penalties for not abiding by the rules of engagement were more stringent. When you are African American and positioned for excellence, there is more scrutiny.

Living life in the public eye requires a tremendous amount of sacrifice. Many times this meant questioning my decisions before making them with regard to how they could affect the family's reputation. I have witnessed both my father and grandfather be reserved in how they have dealt with situations. In these times, it is safe to say that they chose to take the long view, over making a quick decision that seemed expedient in the short-term. Both my grandfather and my father determined that legacy was always more important than anything that they may have faced at the moment.

Civil Discourse

Much of our family engagement yielded great principles in civil discourse. We would sit around the dinner table and talk about current affairs and updates regarding leaders in our community. We learned to speak freely about politics and political issues. We learned that it is appropriate for everyone to construct some opinions about the world and the way in which it should be governed. That is not the case in all families. Not everyone feels comfortable amidst discussions about politics. Some feel that exchanges that are politically rooted can cause an argument or create conflict. There is, however, a way to do so that is more about ideas and patterns of thought. Moreover, even if two or more people in a discussion do not share the same point of view, there is a way to exchange ideas without strife.

Civil discourse is not always exercised, but it should be. It is not possible for each of us to share the same opinion about every issue or interest. The differences that we feel have the potential to make us stronger and smarter as we encompass a vast array of perspectives. The one thing that we all share, regardless of race, creed, or culture, is that we are all a part of the human race. The most prolific aspect of civil discourse that we were taught was always to consider a person's humanity first.

My father would always say: "There are at least three sides to every story. Your side, their side, and the truth. You can believe that you are one hundred percent right, but that doesn't mean that you are right about the whole situation. The truth is the truth, and it is usually found somewhere in the middle."

We were taught to always be pleasant to people, without regard to whether or not we shared the same opinions politically, or in any other sector for that matter. We were advised that we never knew whom we might run into again. Over the years, I have learned that there are strength and wisdom in being temperate with your responses to people. It is good to give yourself time to think about what they are saying as well as provide the other person with the time needed to hear what you are saying. We can sometimes respond to a situation with short-sightedness, primarily when we react in impulse, but taking the long view in situations is not an act of weakness, it is an act of humility and strength.

The Closer

i.   Harvard

In the fall of 1994, I embarked upon my first semester at the Harvard University John F. Kennedy School of Government. Excited to embrace my graduate studies and make my mark, I studied hard and prepared intently each day. After a few weeks, I began to hope that the accelerated pace that we were introduced to would ease once we had demonstrated ourselves to be proficient and productive. I soon recognized that the workload was increasing, instead of leveling. Eventually, the pace became my new normal. I was no stranger to studying long hours, but my discipline and determination were now being stretched to new dimensions. At Harvard, there is no such thing as an academic comfort zone and we were all better students for it. Amidst the toil, my classmates forged tremendous bonds of friendship and mutual respect. After all, we were there in the "fire" together.

The prestige of Harvard attracted world leaders and thought innovators, and exposure of this magnitude was largely impactful for me both personally and professionally. The Forum was where world-renowned speakers and leaders addressed the student body. Seeing people who had dared to change the world, up close and personal, was both energizing and awe-inspiring to me.

I have always believed in the protection of the First Amendment, and I exercise my right to protest wisely. During my second year at Harvard, I became the head of the Black Student Caucus. At that time, there was great focus and debate on a book called *The Bell Curve: Intelligence and Class Structure in American Life*. The book was written by psychologist Richard J. Herrnstein and political scientist Charles Murray. The text argued that intelligence is influenced by the attributes that we inherit as well as the environmental factors that surround us. The book sparked controversy as it implied that certain people of color have lesser Intelligence Quotient (IQ) levels than other ethnicities. As the head of the African American student organization on campus, I worked cross-culturally with Latino students, Asian students, Native American students and other student groups who also found that the book contained some problematic suppositions. This effort provided me with the opportunity to work collaboratively with students of color, which I found to be personally enriching and stimulating.

By the summer of 1995, I was hired as a summer analyst in the Office of Management and Budget. Bill Clinton was in office as the President of the United States. As a summer Budget Analyst, my job was to review how the dollars were allocated to various

Justice Department programs and to gain perspective on how much we were spending. A key component of this work was my ability to ask questions that forced us to consider if we should have been spending more? Was the money allocated having an actual impact? How many people were the dollars actually reaching? Although this was not my favorite line of work, it forced me to see beyond the numbers. Being on the staff of the Executive Office of the President also meant that we received invitations to many of the activities at the White House. When the then President of South Korea came for an official state visit, the staff was invited to attend the welcome at the White House. On the 4th of July, in 1995, the staff received an invitation to watch the fireworks on the White House lawn, with a view of the Washington Monument. This view provided an extraordinary vantage point from which to enjoy a fireworks display! I knew that I had discovered my calling. Many might argue that public service does not pay as well as the private sector; however, the afforded opportunity to bear witness to moments in history that most people will never see is priceless. Most importantly, this work is impactful and purposeful in the lives of others. A greater purpose makes a positive impact, and it is our reason for existence.

As a Harvard graduate, I know without question that Harvard prepared and challenged us to make the most impact wherever and whenever we felt compelled to take action. Harvard made a promise to prepare us to be agents for change, and that promise was honored. Harvard was an impactful reminder that there is power in the individual strengths, gifts, and talents that we possess. We were challenged and required to hone those skill sets while being exposed to practical opportunities that cultivated and prepared us to go out into the world and be impactful. I had every intention of being intentional about how I planned to be impactful. What I knew for certain was there was much work to be done, and I was prepared to roll up my sleeves and dive into the challenges.

ii.   Business Ventures

I have been enamored by business since I was eight years old. For Halloween, I would dress up as a business lady with a briefcase. I did not make the association at the time, that entrepreneurship was calling my name.   Aside from my grandparents and family members, I did not know many business owners. In the black community, people often encouraged us to choose a profession, like being a doctor, lawyer, teacher or a nurse. What I did not realize was how much information I was acquiring about business by simply being in an environment where business was conducted on a continual basis.

When I was twelve, my grandfather allowed me to work for him in his private, swimming lessons business. He taught me how to make phone calls, purchase supplies, and write receipts. Once I remember him getting on my case about proper telephone etiquette. He corrected me and then redirected me to answer the phone and say, "This is the Mickle Residence, how may I help you?" That was one of those unforgettable moments that we had, and I've appreciated him for it. He made me recognize that I had the responsibility of creating a positive image for the caller on the other end by the way I answered the phone. The phone call that I would be responsible for was the first contact that a potential customer would have with the business. Those lessons stayed with me as a little girl, and they have never departed from my way of thinking regarding entrepreneurship as an adult.

While in high school, I had an after-school job working at the local community college library as a circulation desk assistant. I was responsible for checking books in and out and reshelving books. I learned the Dewey Decimal System, and I also fell in love with the experience of being in the library stacks. It was that after school job that taught me to be responsible and to be organized. I began to recognize that much of my family's foundation and lessons that were taught were rooted in attributes to achieve success in entrepreneurship.

My family believed that a person's word should be that person's bond. This philosophy served as a constant reminder that if you said you would do something, you would do everything in your power to ensure that your word came to fruition. This reflection of character, this act of building trust with your friends, constituents, customers, and others demonstrate one's commitment to the virtue of integrity and their reputation. Not only do we need to maintain these values today from a moral perspective, but they are also the best business practices.

Mickle and Associates

I ventured out into the world of entrepreneurship for the first time when I was in my twenties. Mickle and Associates was a fundraising firm, established to assist non-profit organizations with grant writing to find funding for their projects. I was great at finding scholarships for college and grants, and I knew that I could discover success in this space. I saw that there was a problem, and I had the skill set to discover a resolve. Not for profits and businesses would hire me, and I was willing to do the work to assist them in discovering what they needed to conduct their business. The hard work and countless investments of time taught me that, despite my best efforts and qualifications, I was not going to make money overnight.

This was a hard lesson, and for a moment in time, I believe that the notion depressed me. When I first opened the doors of my business, I did not have money coming in, but I was almost certain that if I opened the business, and produced and sent out marketing materials, the people would come. I assumed that people would automatically want to do business with me because I was qualified and a good person, but I soon learned that a profitable business is not guaranteed. There are so many elements to be factored into the results that ultimately yield success.

After some time had passed, I managed to land my first contract and my first check. While I was thrilled at the prospect that it could all happen, I ultimately later made the decision to prepare for and focus on law school instead. I resolved that focusing on my academic achievement had been one area of my life that I had the ability to somewhat predict the outcomes.

The Government Shutdown and the Birth of Mickle Public Affairs

On September 30, 2013, the United States government shut down. It was also the day that we were put on furlough. I remember leaving a meeting with the Chief of Staff who said to our entire staff, "Don't worry about this, we will get it worked out." I felt my stomach sink in that moment, and I realized that my good government job was not as stable as I had once thought it to be. That same day, I had a meeting with a person that I had recently met at a National Urban League Convention. She was a business/life coach. I scheduled a consultation with her and mentioned in passing that I had been thinking of starting a new business. The shutdown lasted for about two and a half weeks.

During that time, I made the decision to go to Houston to visit my brother, Stephan. I had always told him that I wanted to visit Joel Osteen's church during one of my visits. About a week later, my time came, and I was so excited to be in such a warm and impactful church. While in service, they initiated a prayer call. Because of my concerns about the government shutdown, I went down to pray with a prayer partner. While in his presence, I told him that I worked for the Federal Government and that my job had been affected by the shutdown. I explained that I was in need of prayer. This man, whom I had never met, started to pray for me. The more he prayed, the more the word contracts kept coming out of his mouth. This happened so much until he stopped in the middle of the prayer and said, "I'm sorry, ma'am, but God keeps giving me the word contracts." We were both puzzled. What I knew for certain was that if I were at a job receiving a paycheck and W-2's, I would not need contracts. God was trying to tell me something.

The government reopened, and we were all free to return to work. I had experienced a shift internally. Moving into a place of obedience allowed me to recognize that the question for me was no longer "if" I would walk away from my job, but how and when? I embarked upon another period of saving my money, not overcommitting myself and not assuming any new roles. I was not certain of God's plan for me, nor did I know what He was preparing for me. I did know that I wanted to be free to pursue whatever it might be.

Prior to taking the unprecedented leap of faith, I began to do two things. The first was to observe the world around me more closely and come to a better understanding of the needs and problems to be addressed, met, and solved. The second was to pray for my next move. I concluded that God knew what would happen next, and I trusted that God would keep me from making the wrong choice as I had requested. I also began applying for various jobs. God closed every door that was not for me. Believe me when I say that this time of uncertainty did not feel good. During moments such as these, I remained in prayer, even when I experienced hurt, as I watched the doors close. My ego would remind me that I was the General Counsel to a United States Senator, and yet I was not seeing many job offers. The few opportunities that were coming my way had absolutely no appeal to me. Taking one of these positions would have meant the absence of challenge and passion. This was all confirmation that God was calling me to walk away from my job. In 2014, I closed the door on my successful career with the United States. Senate and welcomed the move to entrepreneurship through Mickle Enterprises.

Mickle Enterprises was established by my grandparents in 1957, and it became the foundation upon which many family business ventures were built. In addition to her typing business, my grandmother had a notary service. My grandfather did custom tailoring and alterations and also taught private swimming lessons as part of the various business ventures under the umbrella of Mickle Enterprises. Other ventures included lawn care and real estate. Entrepreneurship was a varied and natural part of our family's fabric. My uncle began a veterinary business and later on, my brother began tutoring students in math. For us, entrepreneurship was a simple, yet powerful act with positive lasting effects.

Some time passed after the government shutdown and my subsequent departure from the U.S. Senate, and Mickle Enterprises soon gave birth to yet another family business, mine, Mickle Public Affairs Agency. Mickle Public Affairs Agency builds on all of the branches of the extensive, legal, public policy and communication experiences that I have acquired over the years. Having performed extensively in governmental writing, in legal consultations, legislatively and from a media perspective, this was the next logical step. Today, we work with trade associations, political candidates, political action committees, and businesses who want to make people aware of their opinions and perspectives and those in need of public relations support. We also work with people who are currently running and those who aspire to run for office. Our role is to make sure that they are communicating effectively with their constituents.

iii.   Establishing Vision

Believe in Yourself

When I think of one difference between working for others and working for myself, I quickly identify the need to have a different level of self-confidence. When you work for yourself, your name is on the line, and you will develop it quickly knowing that success or failure will depend on you. As a business owner, there are many days that make you question if you measure up to your competition, and on other days you wonder if you have what it takes to accomplish the dream that only you can see. Success demands that there is the presence of some intrinsic force that compels you to keep going. The hard truth is that no matter how large your support system is, there will be moments when you are standing alone in the mirror, and you have to be the voice of reason. Entrepreneurship can sometimes be a lonely destination, but the prize is learning about yourself and what motivates you to be the best version of yourself. The goal is to believe in yourself so much, that others are left with no choice, other than to believe in you too.

Believe in What You are Selling

It is possible to sell a product or service in which you do not believe, but why would you opt to do so? In a time when innovation is as vast as the wind, we are all blessed with the opportunity to conceive and bring into fruition the concepts of our wildest imagination. You can create what you wish to have and solve the problems that your business or brand can answer. All things considered, it is a must that you believe in what you are selling if you want others to believe in it. Beginning with an offering of something of value is key. There is not a person who walks the earth that does not have some problem that needs to be solved on their behalf. Not one of us wants to have to think through solving every problem that arises. In this day and time, we sometimes want to leave the house and have someone else, who knows our name, to serve us a cup of coffee. The possibility is very real that solution inventors exist and might be found in the nearest Starbucks. It is not impossible to meet someone who wants to see that every woman regardless, of her size, achieve a svelte figure in her dress. Spanx solutions are the name of the game in business.

Commit to Learning

You cannot possibly know everything. When you work for yourself, you are responsible for. You take out the trash, order the paper clips, shred the papers, and greet customers at the door. In many instances, if you want things done a certain way, you have to do them yourself until you can train or hire someone who is skilled at the proficiency and is producing at the needed level. Being an entrepreneur forced me to learn things I never knew that I needed to know.

One of my first big expenditures as a business owner was to have an amazing website built. I went all out, and I wanted every bell and whistle. The site had to be outstanding and a true reflection of the business that I had worked so hard to assemble. To achieve this end, I hired a web designer. My new company website was all that I had dreamed it would be until the first maintenance item surfaced. I did not realize that the maintenance and updating of the site would require additional assistance and additional funding. When I contacted the web designer to make a request, the designer told me that it was not really his job. He also advised me to hire a web or tech person to be responsible for the maintenance. In that moment, I recognized that at the very least, I had to learn some basic things about website maintenance or incur additional expenses on a consistent basis. You have to prioritize your expenses. I had to learn some things that I never knew I needed to know as well as reserve time and resources to fill in the gaps so that I could really be successful and thrive.

Cost

Analyzing the cost of your business is an ongoing activity. Understanding the proper amount of working capital that you need to adequately provide your services and earn an income from it, requires careful thought and much of your attention as a business owner. There is not one set way to arrive at this cost, which is why no one truly ever tells you. Costs, such as marketing, supplies, contractors, and the list continues, must be factored into the equation. The goal is to be profitable and reinvest funds back into your business to grow it to its full potential. For many, this even comes at the cost of foregoing a personal paycheck to get the business started. Whatever you do, remember to never compare yourself to anyone else, your journey is all your own.

Business Acumen

Although painful, I would venture to say that the best business lessons are gleaned by trial and error. No matter how much education and training you might have received, there are some lessons that are only learned through experience and mentorship. I have lost money on bad business deals, on clients that did not pay their bills, on workers who did not want to show up to work, and on those who did not believe in a full days work for a full days pay. In retrospect, the entrepreneurial process is what has taught me how to identify elements of my business that require my attention and how to best manage the many responsibilities that manifest as a result of being a leader of an entrepreneurial endeavor.

<u>Support</u>

There were people that I thought would support my entrepreneurial pursuits and do business with me who did not. People I had worked with and for, friends, and even family members did not support me. In some cases, I was even told that I was crazy for leaving that "good government job."

Although not verbalized, I felt that there were also people who thought to themselves that they would not slander my efforts to run a successful business, but they also would not be willing to lift a finger or a helping hand to assist. Some will just watch and see how you do on your own, and they will check to see if you fail according to the imaginary standard that they might have constructed in their minds.

I assumed some would say with ease, "Can I do something to help you?" Many did, but some did not. In some ways, I'm glad that everyone has not been a supporter because it has made me even more determined to succeed. To the contrary, there were people whom I would have never guessed who have supported me. Those who sent me business, and prayed for me blew my mind.

In all things, it is important that we count our blessings. I had aunts who helped me set up my office and a cousin that came and assisted me by working on clerical projects for a week. That was huge. At the time, I was a one-woman band, a solo entrepreneur, the chief cook and bottle washer. Life and business are better when you have a team working together. When I have others to share the ups and downs with me, I feel more confident, and I appreciate the moral support.

I was also blessed in that my sister, Amy, has an Economics and Accounting Degree and background, as well as an MBA. Early on, she helped me set up critical financial systems, accounting, and payroll. I recognize the importance of saying "thank you" to those who did not support me, as well as to those who did. They all taught me valuable lessons about being a successful businesswoman.

iv.   Excellence Has No Color

We do not all start at the same place in life. We all face obstacles that are case specific to the economical, environmental, and emotional hands that we are dealt. These obstacles vary in intensity and cannot be measured in terms of equality. While we may not be able to legitimately quantify these factors, it is imperative that we acknowledge the fact that the presence of inequality is a real thing. In spite of this truth, we have no excuse that should hinder us from striving for greatness in our actions, ambitions, and toil. What we do know is that we all possess an internal, decision-making mechanism that has the power to overcome obstacles. Although this feat requires tremendous willpower, there is nothing that is impossible.

If a person is not able to overcome those obstacles as a child, the pilgrimage into adulthood can be seen as a transfer of power. From there, the decisions made are ones that we must own. Turning eighteen can be the great equalizer. Because we have witnessed an abundance of scenarios in which people overcame tremendous obstacles to become the hero or heroine of their own lives, we must adopt the prospect of possibility as our truth. Much of the battle is understanding the institutionalized and societal imposed obstacles that make the playing field uneven from the beginning. In most instances, to overcome anything, we must identify it with a clearly defined compass.

Education

All schools are not created equal. This means that the disparaging disparity that is far too often swept under the rug in our country is a real thing. We could use the disparity as a basis for the argument that not as many students from low socioeconomic environments thrive. This is a valid stance. The key is to discover solutions that are available to combat the problem. We must find ways to leverage what we do have available. There is an abundance of free resources that go unused from government-funded programs to local libraries, social services, literacy organizations and the like. There are many untapped resources that exist. In this same light, we must acknowledge that personal obstacles, that bind us, detract from our ability to access said resources. If I am a person who lives in a house with someone who is negative, and I constantly have to listen to someone telling me how I will never amount to anything, the value of an education is diminished. If I am berated, this negative messaging can evolve into a personal obstacle for me, if I allow it. For someone in an environment such as this, it must be acknowledged that such a challenge is harder to overcome. A child who is dependent upon an adult who slanders efforts to better himself or herself is at a notable disadvantage in comparison to a child reared in a home that encourages and promotes efforts to achieve.

Excellence in Business

There is also a persistent and prevalent stereotype about black-owned businesses. A lot of times, people have come to expect that black-owned businesses are less qualified, less organized, less professional, and of a lesser quality than businesses owned by other ethnic groups. Unfortunately, there are African Americans that take advantage of the stereotype. Some might say that clients or customers should just expect less because of these stereotypes. I flatly reject that notion. This is an excuse for a lack of the presence of excellence. As a business owner, if you know that your employees do not know how to speak to people with friendliness and courtesy, do not put them on the phone as the first line of contact with new employees. If your employees have proven to be frequently late, do not put them in charge of opening the business or perhaps reconsider whether they should remain at all.

Why would anyone want to be in business with low standards? If you do not wake up in the morning with the intent to give your customers the best experience that they can have with you, why be in business? If the commitment is to be anything other than excellence in customer service, I challenge you to reconsider whether entrepreneurship is for you. While it may be true that businesses of color do not always have the same access to startup and working capital that other businesses may have, excellence in other areas of business is not optional.

Your Circle

The best way to be excellent is to surround yourself with it. People who maintain standards of excellence in their own lives cannot be optional along your journey to success. The person that you can learn from may not look like you. Find people who are excellent in the way in which they relate to people, how they manage their finances and conduct their business. Spending time with people who are better than you in a given arena of life can only help you to get better. If we are the sum of the five people that we spend the most time around, then we must seek those who operate in excellence at all costs. Accordingly, we must work to filter everything that does not thrive amidst the same realm of possibilities. Time is the one resource that we cannot recover. It is not replenished nor restored; therefore, we must use every moment to the fullest by walking with those who want the best for themselves and the world in which we live.

Technology

Information is at our fingertips. We have YouTube, social media, e-books, blogs, and audio-books because we are fortunate enough to live in a country where information is abundant and much is free. Technology makes it possible for you to learn from someone that you have never met. You can listen to a TED Talk that they gave, read a book that they wrote. Much of what is available is inexpensive and does not require a lot of costs. Money spent on self-improvement is the sum of the best money that you can spend. There is so much information out there that you can have a virtual mentor or role model that never even knew you existed. You can learn and glean the wisdom and knowledge that they have to offer. I have mentors that I have yet to meet. Choose to surround yourself with people who have excellent habits, and expect you to be your best.

Excuses

We all make excuses from time to time. Regardless of what measuring stick we use to define our excellence, we must be very clear about how excellence is categorized. Using every opportunity and resource that we have access to is critical. When we discover the absence of resources and exposure, we must continue to find innovative ways to create our own. There is no progress in the absence of pressure, but what we know for certain is that we have all been created with something inside of us that has the power to push the envelope to do what we will. We have the power to be a manifestation of our wildest imagination. In the end, only results and progress can be the antidote for excuses.

A Personal Testament

Our family is a pillar of the community and an example of excellence. There are a lot of theories surrounding what it means to be excellent. As people of color, by what measure do we account for excellence? Are the standards of excellence different for our counterparts who are of other ethnicities? Are we held in the same regard?

I have experienced success because of the excellent habits that I have maintained and employed, even in environments in which I was the minority because of my race, gender or both. Some have dismissed my success, saying that it was just affirmative action, since I grew up during a time when affirmative action was legal. I have participated in and benefited from academic recruitment efforts under such initiatives. Such participation did not make me a less qualified student. I was a student who was a person of color and who was competing for a scholarship.

I also do not believe that our family values that encouraged us to be good citizens, good neighbors, and to study hard were anything outside of being prepared to be sustainable and become good people. We all have a responsibility to treat others well and to strive to reach the highest star that we can, regardless of the color of our skin.

The positions that I have held and clients that I work with in very prestigious places became possible because of the quality of work that I have produced and the gifts, talents, abilities, and skills that I bring to the table. Excellence in how I relate to others came from foundational principles I was taught. Showing up on time, dressing for the job you want, not the job you have, treating people with respect and kindness and setting high standards are tenets we all deserve to possess and bring forward in our lives. There are so many factors that we can't control. I would like to believe that the level of excellence that we aspire to is a manifestation of our actions. We have the ability to determine how much or how little of ourselves we will give to a scenario, relationship, or venture. This is where true power lies.

I am not referring to perfection. Perfection is not excellence. The two are not synonymous. When I speak of excellence, I mean your very best. If you do not have all the skills you need, take a class to better yourself. I take a professional development class weekly. Even now at this stage of my career, I am committed to lifelong learning and to remaining current with industry best practices. What was excellent five years ago may have changed, but excellence is not optional.

The elephant in the room that many are afraid to acknowledge is that as people of color, we have to be twice as good to get half as far. Although this has historically been the perception, it still rings true today. Notwithstanding the truth, we are all responsible for performing at the highest level that we can conceive to maintain standards of excellence. If your standards are not that high, ask yourself why? Regardless of what has occurred in our lifetime, we must acknowledge that life owes us nothing. We must take ownership of the action needed to go out and get everything that we believe that we deserve.

Part II:
Why Women Need to Get Involved

"If you don't have a seat at the table, you are on the menu."

-Stephanie Mickle-

I AM CAPTIVATED by the poem, Our Deepest Fear, by Marianne Williamson. It speaks so eloquently about fears of inadequacy that often fuel the power and strength that hide beneath the depths of our being. As women, we have the capacity to wield unprecedented power, and for some, it is intimidating.

Our most effective and productive outcomes in the political space reflect the life experiences of women, our financial contributions and our values.

Women make up fifty plus percent of the population. It is an incomplete notion to discuss the concept of politics and leadership with women absent from the conversation. Doing so would be a disservice to the political system as we know it.

It is also vital to consider women of color as an integral part of the conversation. When women of color are not considered, their voices are not heard, and their perspectives remain dormant in the essential part of the exchange. Policy discussions about education, immigration, economics, pay disparities, healthcare, agriculture, housing, and product safety are all areas of expertise for women who are seeking to get involved. The expertise of women from every life experience can impact any of the aforementioned topics.

A woman of color, armed with data, could speak on healthcare with a broadened perspective. Many of the chronic diseases like diabetes are much more prevalent in her community. This same degree of insight would not be possible if she were not a part of the conversation because the entry point for healthcare is different for all. A woman of color with a seat at the table could expound upon data results that show and demonstrate the prevalence of serious health issues in her community. Women of color have experienced the effects of diseases like diabetes in their families and in their communities; therefore, they have personal experiences or observations that can be invaluable in the cure and control of problems like diabetes. Women are suffering from

57

heart disease at an alarming rate, and it affects women differently from the way that it affects men. A woman who has either experienced it firsthand or is familiar with the symptoms or criterion that avidly affect women will bring a much-needed perspective from which to advocate and provide insight. Although every person has her respective lens, the argument that defends the need for the lens from which women see the world is crucial as our male counterparts are not excluded in the same ways in which women are.

The omission of women's perspectives in the political and decision-making processes is historically evident and even more so for women of color.

Why Me? Why Politics?

I was born into politics, and I cannot remember a time when it was not a part of the discussions going on around me. I was impacted directly and indirectly. My knowledge base evolved, and my viewpoints matured. As a young girl, I knew that people voted and that the act of doing so was important. My grandparents on my mother's side worked for the NAACP and registered people to vote. Harry T. Moore served as the President of NAACP, in the 1920's and 1930's. His house was bombed because of his mission to empower his people. I had heard the stories and felt the wrath of the inequalities of the world, but I didn't know what to do about them or how to strike the right balance for taking action.

I initially thought that politics was a dirty word. It was the butt of many jokes that people told, Today, I have a much broader understanding of the needs of our country, myself, and the impact of taking action in the political space. I recognize that my interest has always been piqued by the concept of public policy.

Understanding political dynamism helped me to acknowledge that I could change people's opinions about things or make a physical change to the environment around me. Involvement is what allows us to get a school built or assume responsibility for public safety by having a stop sign put up in a neighborhood or a traffic light erected in a dangerous intersection. Public policy has always been intriguing and appealing to me. Engaging in public policy means that change can happen from action.

I have dedicated my life to understanding and taking action to this end. No matter what I've done in my life, it has always woven back into the political space. Even though the political process is imperfect, I love the country so much. To this end, I don't believe that we can face an obstacle too great that we can't get past, even in consideration of those who are not competent in office. However, I know that without the invaluable contributions of women, our process would be deeply flawed. The founders of our country put many mechanisms in place to help us solve problems and maintain balance.

With this in mind, my perspective is that of a long view. Some believe that it takes too long to get things done, but I know with certainty that there are benefits to slowing things down. This is true of life and politics. Each policy or concern must be thoroughly evaluated and investigated to ensure that the public is accurately informed. The slowing of the process in big government or in city politics empowers us to look at ways in which things can be improved, tweaked, or adjusted. The inclusion of women is equivalent to the slowing down of the process and the discovery of balance of power. We need agents of change in the collaborative process of ideas and procedures for the way our country is run. Women are needed to explore why various concepts matter and why we are all required to be involved to realize democracy in its purest form.

When people, politics, and power are on the table, I don't believe any topic to be taboo or off limits. We must deny ourselves the protection of comfort zones for the sake of arriving at an intended destination of awareness, advocacy, and advancement. Intentional exchanges regarding much of the subject matter that we are ashamed, inferior or historically not fit to discuss is a step towards liberty and justice for all. A time when we all can sing America and stand proudly in the promises of our country's forefathers is also the time that women's voices, perspectives, and presence are all made a priority. We will not realize the fullness of our potential until this is not seen as optional but an intricate part of the process.

A. The Real Talk

i. Acknowledging the Absence and Lack of Diverse Representation in the Political Process

Lack of diverse representation in all aspects of the political process is still very much a present reality. Despite our nation's efforts to become a perfect union, oppression still exists in the political process and the workplace. We do ourselves a disservice by not allowing the best and the brightest to emerge and participate, even when they do not look like us. Thus, because a lack of representation does not yield best practices, it must not be tolerated. We must continue to open doors of opportunity for qualified people of color and women who are fully capable of doing the work to make our country better. While I was working in the U.S. Senate, staffers of color had a number of meaningful conversations about the lack of promotions, the lack of opportunities, our experiences as well as instances of white privilege, across the Senate. These perspectives and examples were not limited to any particular Senate committee or member's office. They were related to larger professional diversity and cultural sensitivity issues.

Shortly after I began working in the United States Senate, a black staffer once told me that the Senate was casually known by some as the oldest plantation in the country. I was immediately stunned by that metaphor. It seemed so pejorative. I later learned that what they meant was that the breadth and access to opportunities for people of color in many ways were limited in practice and that their notion was that there were not as many opportunities to advance. After all, a person had to be well prepared to be hired by the United States Senate in the first place. However, the higher a person progressed, the less formal support structures were there, and many times staffers of color were left to figure it out. I do not believe that this experience is solely limited to government. I have heard my friends say the same of their experiences in other industry sectors. This was indeed true in the legal profession. It is important to encourage efforts to support diversity at the more senior levels of the economy and not just for the sake of diversity but maximum productivity. I must admit, that my experience as a senior staffer to a white Senator could be described more as the exception than the rule. I came into the Senate with work experience and three degrees, two of them from Ivy League schools. I came in at a Mid-Senior level and quickly moved up to senior level. That was going to be the only level for me.

For many staffers who were persons of color, the most direct path to becoming a senior staffer was, in many cases, going to work for a Member of Congress who was also a person of color. I saw many staffers of color around the Senate languishing in entry-level or junior level positions while their white counterparts were being promoted over them. It happened enough for me to know and to surmise that this was not just limited to an occasional situation. Eventually, they would advance, or leave the Senate to pursue options that offered them greater career advancement.

I have mentored students from many backgrounds and worked with hundreds of interns throughout my career. I can recall a chance meeting with a young man who previously interned with me while he was a student in college. As we conversed, he plainly stated: "I will always remember you because you were the only person in the office who ever gave me any assignments." He was a very bright African American man, and I was startled to learn that of the thirty plus people eligible to give him an assignment in the office, I was the only one who did. I did my best to make sure that the African American interns had research assignments from me so that their internships were of substantive value, and did not just consist of running errands. Many young people see the value in working on Capitol Hill to increase their territory, establish political roots and build substantial connections, and I gave assignments to all students whom I believed had the initiative and the drive to learn and excel. It is my hope that this same mindset becomes our reality throughout the political realm.

ii. The Many Reasons that Women are Not Involved in the Political Process

Underserved, underprivileged, undermined and most importantly underrepresented. From a bird's eye view, an onlooker could be led to believe that women have either selectively chosen or they have been selectively disregarded in reference to the political process. It is valid to question the disposition of women and especially women of color in our country. Are our voices heard? Are our perspectives considered? Who leads the charge for the most pressing issues concerning our civil rights, dignity, and progression? Whom can we turn to in an attempt to define our futures? It is imperative for women to carefully examine the various reasons for the lack of women representation in politics. This examination must exist to determine ways to bridge the invisible gap that serves as a barrier from the perspectives and viewpoints that represent over half of the population. As women, we too sing America.

Major Obstacles for Women Wanting To Lead

Whether making the decision to lead or being led by internal motives to assume responsibility for a given scenario, or the predetermined set of outcomes, women can face multitudinous obstacles in the face of leadership. To thoroughly examine the effects and limitations of the challenges, it is imperative for us to carefully consider each in context.

Lack of Examples

When you are the only person who looks like you in a room, it can drive the perception that you do not belong or that your presence is not worthy. Historically speaking, many of the campaign managers, finance directors, and with certainty, the candidates have not often been women or people of color. In a time when progression is trending, it is still hard to believe that we must consider this as truth. Lack of visual representation feeds the perception that there is a lack of an actual presence. Being different, working while being misunderstood, feelings of isolation and rejection are all contributing factors that make the prevalence of women in these arenas scarce. Let us consider that Michelle Obama had never seen a black first lady. She looked for a way to learn the role and brought her essence and image of goodness into the position. She made her experience impactful for the rest of the world to now see it possible. She is not different from anyone else. As women, we all have the power to be the example that we need to see. It takes high determination and an unwillingness to allow limitations. The more we find ways to get involved and create our pathways and avenues to join the discussion, the more we increase our opportunities for representation and diversification in the playing field.

Traditions of Political Parties

Some might find it controversial in thought, but there is a great deal of money, time and effort that goes into keeping certain jobs in the political arena reserved for white men. We have all heard about the inclusion of writers of color in Hollywood and the music industry, but how often do we discuss the lack of diversity amongst the political parties, especially the Democratic Party? This train of thought goes far beyond the surface level discussions about the diversity of the faces that you see aligned with a political party in particular. I suggest that there is a grave deficit in the diverse candidates enlisted to run on behalf of these parties, to do business with the parties and to hold positions of power within the parties. This poses a tremendous problem as each of these players informs and impacts the political process in real and tangible ways that ultimately affect voters and constituents.

For example, when you examine how campaigns are mapped out, a traditional model is constructed in such a way that there is less emphasis placed on minority outreach efforts before the primary. In many instances, political campaign leaders may not say so publicly, but their actions reflect that they do not believe it is worth the time, money or energy. In hindsight, it is a missed opportunity to fundraise and hear from a constituency with valuable perspectives and support. It is a missed opportunity to develop relationships of value to the process.

Similarly, if you have ever visited a predominantly black church during election season, it is likely that you have witnessed a political candidate visit on the Sunday before the election. The candidate may want your vote, not because they have taken the time to get to know the parishioners personally or their issues of concern, but simply because they are of a particular political party. In many instances, they get some of those votes. To this end, I would be remiss if I failed to acknowledge that there is an assumption in some circles about what black voters do and how vital they are to the election process. I am not basing the expression of these thoughts on assumption; these sentiments are as a result of personal experiences.

There is a dichotomy of viewpoints when a woman is also a person of color. Some describe this as the concept of a double minority. In many instances in politics, the voting block defined as "women" is defined as white women. However, there is a vast diversity within women, just as there is within all populations. This is significant because women of color bring their life experiences from their respective ethnicities and backgrounds to the political arena and the legislative policy forum. At all costs, women must intentionally determine the next steps and series of actions towards establishing a presence as we see fit. The way in which we categorize appropriate representation for women of color must be the result of a collective effort and mindset. Discovering unity, and running for office are impactful ways to ensure that we are present and represented.

Money

As a collective, there is much work to be done when it comes to fundraising. Women have to learn how to fundraise in such a way that we have the financial leverage to have a seat at the table. Fundraising in this manner will only come with a team that reflects the diversity of thought and approach, and it should not look like the political status quo. As women, we must hold candidates accountable for our money. If candidates determine themselves to be leaders and want our votes and our money, then they need to represent what is critical to our interests. Women have not always been willing to have that conversation, but it is time.

The Learning Curve

Historically, women have been an intricate part of the political process, but the imagery is not nearly as prevalent. Even today, I would venture to say that many women do not personally know any other women involved in the political process. It is possible that even in our churches and communities, we might not be familiar with one person who holds an office. If this is the case, this can also mean that many of us are farther removed from politics than those who engage with people who are a part of the process on a regular basis. This means that we are farther away from the issues that most impact us and farther away from utilizing our skill set to bring about change. If you do not have any politicians or political junkies in your peer groups to dissect the most pressing issues in your community or anyone who can help you find answers and understanding, then there are many topics that you could be addressing that are slipping through the cracks, right in your neighborhood, city, state, and country. This empty void comes with a tremendous opportunity in favor of those who are most familiar with the ebbs and flows of the political process, and it serves as a tremendous learning curve for those who are unfamiliar.

Men have observed other men engage in politics since the birth of our nation and even before in other civilizations worldwide. The imagery of such great speeches and debates, legislation, treaties, and declarations come readily to mind. For men, having such a base of experiential knowledge has yielded lasting effects.

That said, all is not lost, ladies. Politics is not nuclear physics or impressionist art, but it does have rules, laws, and fluidity to it like any great masterpiece.

The good news is that it does not matter where you are in your journey, you can make a difference. Believe it or not, you might be missing an invaluable opportunity to get involved, right where you are, with the current skill set that you have. Maybe you haven't realized that there is something that you want and desire to do. Many people say they are not good at politics or anything new and unfamiliar, and many are afraid to venture out because they don't have a support system in place to show them the way. The key is demystifying the process and recognizing an area of need that you can offer of yourself. If no one has ever told you, the world needs you to get involved in the political space now.

It's Not for Me

Consider the subjects of science and math. On far too many occasions, girls have been made to feel that they don't have strengths in these subjects. What that says to me is that we need to push harder to ensure that there is not the presence of a deficit. The bigger questions that we should be asking ourselves are: "Have we been challenging girls in science and math?", and "Have we made sure that they have the necessary resources to be successful in these fields?" The imagery of scientists and mathematicians points to the success of men. Hidden Figures was a miraculous depiction of women who excelled in both math and science and how their contributions changed the trajectory of the nation's technological advancements. We are meant to exercise our brilliance in every field conceivable. A parallel can be drawn to politics. Women have been led to believe in many ways that it's a man's world. The reality is that we all need each other. The presence of women in politics and leadership is necessary now, and it will become more necessary as we embrace diversity in all areas of life.

As a woman, when you see only men in the governor's office in your home state, you might get the impression that you do not belong there, but you do. As little girls, we are taught that specific roles are reserved for boys, but this is not the case with politics. We must all challenge these notions. The more women assume positions of leadership, the more we empower future generations through imagery and examples. The moment we take ownership of the narrative defines the moment we can continue in the establishment of examples of women who lead. It begins and ends with us. When we ponder, who should be leading the charge, we need not look far. The reflection in the mirror, says it all; it begins and ends with us.

Getting Used

We have seen candidates whose presence was promoted as the face of a campaign with very little genuine support for their success as an elected official. In some instances, women were simply the window dressing for all of the men in the actual business of the political process. Women need to be articulating their perspectives and offering substantive policies and ideas to make a change. Beauty, like knowledge, is a form of power. However, we as women have far more to offer than eye candy to attract some and distract others. There are real issues at hand and lives on the line.

Stereotypes|Judgments

Scrutiny is inevitable for any candidate or leader, and it is one reason many shy away. I believe anything worth having is worth the fight to get it. Women and men who decide to lead are placed under intense microscopes. Women are often forced to question whether they have the perfect family structure, what their clothing and hairstyles communicate, their sexual preferences, and a list of other factors that have very little to do with their ability to serve or lead. This factor of judgment and scrutiny keeps many women on the sidelines. The unwarranted attacks and scrutiny on a person's attributes or choices can have adverse effects on some. Funding might pose another concern for some women. It takes money to fund a campaign, therefore; research, creativity and involving others will be crucial to beginning the process. This is why I offer that there are no limits to how or where women can lead. We cannot allow the fear of scrutiny hinder us or detour us from our pursuits. We must believe that where there is a will; there's a way.

Power Dynamics

In the past, some of what I have said in this book would have been categorized as confrontational and possibly even controversial. I promised myself that when I wrote this book, I would express authentically, what others may not be able to communicate. Many of the purest sentiments of our hearts have been hidden for fear of being victimized by the undercurrent of white supremacy and misogyny. On so many occasions, as people who are different, other, marginalized, however, one might choose to describe it, we have oppressed our thoughts and hidden them from the world for fear that by publicly declaring these truths would compromise our livelihood or the safety of our children. We have long since known that too much chatter can pose a threat to safety. We have seen in days passed, and it still rings true today. Social media has changed the scope of our perspectives in many ways. We are witnessing the emergence of new generations of people and voters who are not afraid to acknowledge, with the conviction that we need more people in positions of power that look like us or have a similar life experience. More and more people are publicly inquiring how it is possible to have comprehensive and effective advocacy by those who do not experience life through a similar lens?

Stereotypes

The stereotypes that women are subjected to in the political arena are no different than what we face in society at large. The list of stereotypes is never-ending, ranging from historically biased assumptions to fabricated notions of imaginary standards by which these perceptions are conceptualized. The identification and challenge of these assumptions lead us to a distressing but vital conversation to dissect these stereotypes and their impact on women's ability to lead respectively.

Too Aggressive

If a woman speaks about the truest sentiments of her mind with passion, she might be labeled too aggressive. Given this same passion and a different package, it is possible that this same behavior would be categorized as passionate or assertive.

Weight and Appearance

Much like many other areas of discussion, it is not a sound practice to assume that one set of standards fits all. Society has embedded notions of self-hatred in an attempt to demean and demolish our perceptions of self-worth and self-esteem while subjecting women to certain standards of beauty and body type.

The stereotypes for women of color are more far-reaching. Should a woman be penalized and deemed not a valid voice in the political process for having wide hips and a big butt? Should a woman with a petite frame be penalized? No. These attributes should have no bearing on a woman's ability to lead or to be considered for positions of influence.

Women face so many obstacles regarding physical appearance on a daily basis. It is a grim reality that these factors, in addition to weight, must be considered when deciding how and whether to engage in the political process. Women are characterized by their clothing, sexuality, and grooming, but that is the way it has always been in all professions. Is it fair and realistic? No, it isn't fair, but it is realistic.

The Twice As Good Rule

As a woman, your mere presence and participation in political discussions are still considered by many somewhat unusual and atypical. Therefore, you must prove yourself worthy of even having a presence in the room, a voice in the conversation, or an opinion in the matter, by being twice as good. Inequality in pay, lack of representation in positions of leadership, being second-guessed or undermined while attempting to lead are also startling realities that often accompany the process for women to lead and engage in the political process.

Historical Discrimination

The longstanding history of discrimination against women is another factor that women considering getting involved in the political process must face. Many correlations can be drawn to instances in which women, particularly women of color, are perceived as a threat. Perceptions are formed by virtue of the things that we do, the way that we interact, the je ne sais quoi that makes us interesting and fascinating as women. Historical discrimination could be due, in part, to not being understood, respected or fully appreciated.

Lack of Opportunities

You do not know what you do not know. If you are not at the golf course or in the room when people are making decisions and making selections, then you are not included in the strategy nor decision-making process. No matter how much we are held accountable for paving the way for ourselves, we must acknowledge that the opportunities presented are at a much smaller scale and consistency versus that of our counterparts. This is a deficit that poses a threat to the involvement of women in the political process.

Colorism

I refuse to pretend that the color of one's skin is insignificant when addressing the factors regarding the imbalance of women of color in leadership positions. Whether we like it or not, people are selected for opportunities based in part on the way that they appear. Although this is not the only factor, it is a factor nonetheless. If someone likes the way you look, and you are qualified, and you are easy to be around, chances are, you stand a better chance at being selected over someone who does not meet the societally imposed criteria and who challenges the status quo on various issues. This is all about socialization. If I compare my resume with that of a woman who is dark-skinned, and we have the same credentials, is it possible that my lighter complexion could give me an advantage? It is possible, perhaps subliminally, but such concepts lurk. If you look across the spectrum of women of color in leadership, there is a range of skin tones and complexions, and there should be. After all, skin shade has nothing to do with our ability to serve and to lead. Moreover, if this is the case, why are opportunities for women of color so scarce?

FEAR: Are Women Afraid to Engage?

It was brought to my attention, on several occasions, that I was one of two African American women in the history of the Senate to serve as General Counsel. I did not take that opportunity for granted, and I considered it a blessing. While that was true, it could not answer the calling that was placed on my life to serve in other capacities.

If you know that there is a calling that you cannot get out of your mind, even if you try to ignore it, and it moves you towards action, that means that you are supposed to be doing it. Sometimes you have to have courage from the depths of your soul. Even in the scariest moments when faith at least the size of a mustard seed is required, there is nothing worse than regret. It is my hope that no woman departs this life, saying, "I should have spoken out, or I should have taken action." I implore you to try it. If you decide what you believe you are called to do does not work out, you've learned some things. You've learned that it is not the end of the world, and you have acquired valuable lessons from which to improve future efforts to empower others.

The consequences of immobility are far more significant than trying and not succeeding. What if you made a decision to lead and you discover that you are amazing at it? What if your work results in policies getting changed, and people being positively impacted? Whether you know it or not, you are an effective leader.

We must remember that leadership is not about our agendas; it is about making the world in which we live better. The best leaders are servant leaders. They subscribe to the higher calling. Leadership is most effective when it is about a bigger purpose, and we have all been created with one embedded in us. If I am at home and afraid, then I am not moving forward. If I fail to make a difference in the lives of others, I might live with regret and not be able to find inner peace. We have all heard stories about those living with regret. Take the leap of faith!

Knowledge

It is imperative for a leader to understand her audience. The political space and leadership are not all that different. To be a leader, you must convince people to follow you. To mobilize people and encourage them to advocate for your issues, they must see you as fit to lead. Taking action to this end also means continuous education and dedication to learning about those to be served. Some organizations are proliferating to fill this need. In many instances, there are opportunities available, but the skills needed to do the job are not in place. We must take the initiative. No one is attempting to level the playing field for us; we must be ready, willing and able to do so for ourselves. We have to take the bull by the horn and lead from the front as well as the back. This can only be a reality when we are armed with the most current and cutting-edge information that exists. Take your time, learn the issues and the obstacles. Get up to speed. You do not need to know everything about a particular issue to get started, but you must be serious about what you are doing.

I stand firmly in the belief that there are factors about the environments that we frequent and in those that we want to be recognized as innovators. To the contrary, there are also rules of engagement that we must learn to navigate. No matter how much we decide to put our spin on rules, they are still rules. The more effectively we learn to navigate, the more active we can be in creating a path and opening doors for others. The ultimate goal is to see more women be successful and engaged in their efforts. There is a place for women in the political arena. We just obtained the right to vote a little over one hundred years ago;

therefore, we are not many generations removed from those women who did not have the right to vote.

I am advocating for full participation in the political process by women. We need to be participating in every single way. What I am suggesting does not take all of your time. You can do it during your volunteer time. The most important action that can be taken is to pick a lane or a specific issue and work it. It will be your saving grace to remember that it is not necessary to try to be everything to everybody. Trying to do too much makes us less effective and minimizes our opportunities to get anything accomplished. less effective. As women, it is our nature to build. This same desire that burns deep within our hearts is a clear indicator of the fact that we would build upon our beloved country. There are so many reasons that women must lead and be engaged. It is not in the best interest of our communities for women to refrain from political involvement.

B. I Don't Need Equality, I Already Have It – Silencing the Noise and Closing the Gender Gap

i. Defining Inequality

Inequality is commonly defined in relation to the actions of people. It is situational. For example, I may not have the same opportunities to advance. I may not make the same amount of money as a man. I may not be consulted as frequently for my expertise. I may not be perceived as capable of taking on a particular job like the President of the United States. In the political space, it may be presumed that I am not as strong on national defense issues or human rights issues or even ways and means and appropriation because I am a woman. It may be perceived that I am less likely to be knowledgeable about those things. Maybe, it is perceived that I am "softer" and not firm in my stance on those issues. It is possible that I am left out of the discussion or meeting altogether. Similar experiences exist in other spaces. As a young attorney, I remember an instance where my female colleagues and I were not invited to golfing outings with other attorneys. It was assumed that, as female lawyers, we had no desire to play golf. Maybe we did, perhaps we did not, but we were not invited nor given that opportunity to decide. It was unfortunate as a great deal of business is conducted on the golf course. Such oversights could have meant missed opportunities to network and develop business ventures. Let's discuss how we define inequality and alleviate it at every possible level. We cannot realize the forward progression needed in the political realm without clearly understanding why inequality exists and how to respond in the presence of bias.

Why Does Gender Inequality Exist?

Not only must we acknowledge that inequality exists, but we must also dissect why it exists. For whatever reason, it is human nature to want to make ourselves feel better than others. Whether we like it or not, some men will sometimes subjugate women to feel better about themselves. When men have these or similar sentiments, they limit job opportunities and remain in a mindset of inequality. Men who subscribe to the fact that they are better and feel the need to make individual decisions that keep men on top or put institutions in place to ensure this end create an unavoidable imbalance in every facet of life. In the political space, equality and responsibility must be monitored, and all parties must be held accountable for equity in the governing of policies that impact men, women, and children. What this line of thinking fails to take into account is that women have specific strengths, gifts, and abilities that men do not.

The early feminist waves could be referenced as the obverse. To this end, certain views believed women to be superior to men. This was true to the extent that some people were seeking to reject the presence of men altogether by spelling the word women without the letter "e" and with the letter "y" to extract the word men. Arguments such as the fact that women are better at multitasking, charged with giving birth; holding down a high level, high tech, powerful job and more, set the stage for the depiction of a woman's unprecedented greatness. However, feminism is also a form of gender inequality from my perspective. I am of the opinion that any source of defamation or disregard for one group by another can become a source of bias. Female supremacy is just as harmful as male supremacy. The perception that I am better than you because of having specific innate abilities is no different from the man saying he is better and maintains this by keeping women out of specific spaces. You cannot say that the rain is more important than the sun. They are not the same; both are needed to grow. The goal should not be to incubate environments that foster divides but to cultivate high expectations for the upliftment and performance of all groups.

Self-Imposed Gender Inequality?

It is possible that we create gender inequality through self-selection. It is natural for little boys to want to play with other little boys or little girls to want to play with other little girls. This disposition often carries on into adulthood. There are activities that we naturally seek out socially to engage that are same gender presence, just for comradery or socialization. Also realized in the workplace, the problem that can arise is when there is a belief or perception that this is the only way. There is value in same-gender engagement but only in the absence of discrimination. There are institutions like the Boys and Girls Scouts of America that have existed for years. Recently it was announced that the Boy Scouts would accept girls, although Girl Scouts has not adopted the same policies. It is possible that the Girl Scouts stance was to recognize it as essential to continue in the legacy of the development and cultivation of girls in lieu of inequalities that we often face. Maybe, they believe that it is important to have institutions with this focus. I attended an all-girls college. I understand the value of single-sex institutions and consider them to be powerful. I would not be happy if my alma mater changed its policy to admit all applicants. This is not, however, regarding transgender students. There is value in encouraging entities and groups of a similar nature. Likewise, the existence of fraternities, sororities, single-sex associations, and organizations prove that there is power in the association of like minds and like gender.

ii. Closing the Gender Gap

If you are good at what you do, that is the best way to close the gender gap and encourage others to embrace equality with someone who does not believe in equality or diversity. This holds true in politics, in business, and in leadership. Your actions and the data documenting your performance are your proof. Assuming that people will see the value of your contributions and give you credit for those contributions can be a costly mistake that results in less opportunity for advancement. Making assumptions in the political space can lead to lower pay, lower expectations, and the mindset that constituents know what you have done on their behalf. Likewise, there is a benefit in teaching children at a young age about equality and changing hearts and minds over time. This is an essential milestone towards change.

We must all take note of how we can become advocates and power players in the fight against inequality. Everyone is responsible. It is not possible to remedy the disparities without all hands on deck. An example of this would be pay disparity. No matter what field you are in, pay inequality is valid, and it has been a longstanding concern.

I can recall a point in my life in which I was testing the market for job positions. I had a total of eight job offers coming out of law school. I remember turning down one offer when I learned, inadvertently, that I would not be paid as much as a male counterpart who would also be starting as an entry-level attorney. Shortly after, I received another offer from a different firm; their offer was significantly higher. I asked the firm whether all of the new attorneys received the same offer? The response was "yes," and I was pleased to discover that the firm was committed to the exercise of equality.

As life would have it, I acquired more information that would prove to be insightful. I learned from experience and data that over time the gender inequality for pay often presents itself as a person advances. A man and a woman may start at the same salary, but the pay disparity evolves. This is not a fact in all cases, but it does occur often enough that it poses a significant problem for many. Any pay disparity occurrence is one too many because it impacts a family's economics in the short-term day to day and where generational wealth is concerned. There is a perception that the woman may take off time to start a family, thus diminishing her value to the firm. In consideration of these circumstances, it is also thought that a woman may not be given the same type of assignments that establish her value with the company. The reduction of opportunities to show what you can do for the company can be detrimental in many ways. It can detract from your eligibility for the big bonuses, big raises, and promotions.

Aside from targeted instances of pay inequality, many occurrences are as a result of human nature. As people, we embody our own set of preferences, which also means prejudices. As the owner of the company, you can tell Jim, whom you have hired as your president to treat all employees the same. However, Jim is still human and will likely do what he believes is in the best interest of the company in his role as president. If Jim believes that Fred can do a better job than Sara, because Sara is a mother and has demonstrated a personal interest in her family on the weekends, Jim may be more inclined to select Fred for the job or to carry out the task. This rings true, especially in instances where Jim's pay is directly tied to the performance of the professionals that he has been charged to lead or oversee. It may not be possible always to change people's views, but it is possible to change behavior. Likewise, if a company says, we are going to pay a hiring manager to recruit and retain qualified women, it has now created a situation where there is the establishment of a personal incentive to make choices that align with that directive.

C. Taboo Topics in Public Policy and What to Do about Them- A Case Study #METOO

#METOO - Why do legislative responses and funding appropriations for rape kits, domestic violence shelters, sexual harassment training, sex crimes prosecutions, and programs languish? Why does it seem that politicians do not prioritize these issues in the same way that perhaps other programs are prioritized? After all, one in three women experiences some form of #METOO. Well, I have a theory, and in this arena, it is not just because we need more women elected to office and at the legislative table providing policy guidance. It is also not just because historically, women have been treated as less than equal to men. All of those things are true, yes. Hopefully, learning how to be a great advocate on these particular issues is why some of you have picked up this book.

Consider this. As human beings, we need to define people as all good or all evil. The truth is that we all can act in good faith or act in the absence of all that is good. Why is it that we support the conviction of R. Kelly, famed Rhythm & Blues singer but struggle to unravel the case of Bill Cosby? We have managed to personify Bill Cosby as his fictional character, Dr. Heathcliff Huxtable, star of The Cosby Show. Opposite R. Kelly, many have a harder time believing that it is possible that Dr. Huxtable has an evil bone in his body. To see someone who has done so much good and be classified as evil is hurtful. He has Ph.D.'s, philanthropic endeavors, and has been responsible for countless success stories for people of color through his contributions. The accusations of sexual misconduct, by countless women, does not align with the perceived view of who he is. Moreover, whether we choose to admit it or not, the need to classify each other as good or evil is the reason people struggle with accepting ugly truths that rise to the surface about those whom we've held in high regard. If there is an upstanding member of the community, a doctor, a political change maker, an influencer, we expect to place that person in a box labeled "good" until further notice.

We do ourselves a disservice to say that a person is either good or evil. It behooves us to expand our thinking and subscribe to the notion that we all can operate under either classification. Matt Lauer's and Harvey Weinstein's surfacing indiscretions and sexual violations account expansive coercing in non-consensual sexual situations. America was hesitant to believe in the whisper of the allegations until they became unwanted roars. Harvey Weinstein was a huge Democratic donor as well as the one that gave Malia Obama her internship. How could someone who was responsible for so much good, also be the owner of hands that demean and devalue women? If we examined everyone closely, including ourselves, we would discover more grey areas than expected.

We are witnessing a significant rise in the discussion surrounding rape culture and the opportunity for real policy measures, legislative changes and increases in appropriations exist. Charlamagne, pop culture enthusiast and host of a radio show called The Breakfast Club, discussed that afterthought and reconsideration publicly, he realized that the first time he had sex with his now wife, that it could have been considered non-consensual because she was inebriated. Together, they discussed the incident and in a bold move, pushed the #METOO discussion forward.

In public policy, we cannot afford to allow cultural exchanges such as these to be treated as taboo. Further, as a practical matter, how do we legislate around the flaws of humanity? We legislate by assigning clinical value, statistical validity and practical solutions. We alleviate the sting of intensely personal subjects and ethical and emotional landmines and redirect the focus to legislative and programmatic solutions. Addressing these issues head-on is the only way for #METOO to gain sufficient traction such that minds are changed towards a new level of consciousness. This means as well to treat it like any other policy issue, with tangible definitive rules and concrete action. Doing so does not diminish the persons who experience #METOO; it translates the issues in a way that extends their credence.

This is not to say we cannot be human and empathetic, as women especially. We can help to accept accountability as a society for what we have done to diminish women and men who have come forward with the haunting truths of abuse and aggression exercised towards them and for those who have not done so. Those who ask: "What are people going to think of me?" This series of unfortunate events can leave victims to question their weaknesses or be subjected to the public scrutiny that does the same. To some extent, many victims internalize their victimization through ownership of the experience. Whether the world agrees with the methods, platform or specifics of the #METOO movement, we can recognize that it has opened the forum for meaningful discussion and a community of support for victims to come forward sans the shame. Saying #METOO is synonymous with silencing the shame. We must engage in the difficult conversations. We must silence the shame. We must not make excuses for the assault and degradation of each other.

Unintentional harm in the political space is possibly more hazardous to those in our society at large than the presence of intentional aggression and discriminatory practices.

It chips away at the very fibers established to ensure that all people feel capable and powerful amidst opportunities that lend themselves towards a fair shot at life. These moments are often too subtle to recognize.

Furthermore, society has taught women to diminish #METOO concerns and dismiss them as "boy talk" thereby minimizing the potential harm that failing to address #METOO causes. In other words, silence, failing to understand the speaker's perspective on the comment or action, equal an implied consent. What about the voiceless? What about those who feel as though they do not have a way to address the microaggression that they experience by not seeing their issues advocated for in a way that represents their voice? Well, respectfully, that is where you come in. Where there is a void, there is an opportunity.

We can all increase accountability for the way in which we lead through difficult situations in the #METOO movement. There is no merit in blaming the victim. Just as there is no solution to be found in demanding perfection. On too many occasions, women and men are senselessly victimized by circumstances that are entirely unwarranted and unjustified. In these matters, we must advocate for justice and stand in unity to protect one another.

A final note. Whether we choose to acknowledge this as truth or not, there are also times when women are the aggressors, the assaulters, the abusers of men. As women, we need to recognize triggers that we sometimes use against whomever we might be involved within an exchange. We are all human, and in the midst of a tumultuous situation, most often we are fighting to be heard or to get our side across to the other person, who may or may not be positioned to receive it. This is again in no way, shape or form justifying any behavior that is verbally, emotionally, physically, socially or financially, harmful to another person. I am merely suggesting that we consider all sides of the series of events that we do not will or wish to have occur and to recognize trends or patterns from which to bring about resolve.

Accountability must be examined from a myriad of perspectives, but in all things, to thine own self, be true. To thine public policy, be creative, factual and data-driven.

D. The Cornerstones

The Freedom that we enjoy in the United States of America is not free. Freedom is a luxury that we must pursue and protect. It is something that must not be taken for granted. Recognizing that both political freedom and prosperity have an attached price tag, also means acknowledging that action must be made towards the desired outcome. As citizens, we become most powerful when we recognize that we must take action to protect the freedoms that we enjoy and that we must develop the political currency needed to expand our ability to make changes and to increase our leadership.

i. Cultivating Political Currency

When we consider the term "political currency," we are immediately drawn to the capital that politicians and those involved in the political arena accrue. From mobilizing voters, spearheading initiatives, spreading awareness about the legislature, fundraising; therefore, the list of ways to accumulate political currency is varied. Everything that you do from making phone calls, to scheduling meetings, releasing press statements on issues, building relationships, building strategic alliances are all actions that can establish political currency.

We all have the power and ability to cultivate political currency, but we have to be dedicated and intentional about doing so, just as we do in saving money in our households for a rainy day. There are everyday heroes like yourself who learn about the magnitude and impact of the development of political currency and use it to lead to critical policy issues for their communities and the nation. Political currency is an iron fist that can move mountains towards change and equality when used for good.

Gun Control was an issue that I covered as part of my legislative portfolio responsibilities for Senator Nelson. Because Florida had a season of high profile shootings, my days for a time were filled with learning every aspect of the topic. From the weapons used to the concerns of civil rights groups, it was in my wheelhouse. As a country, we were reeling from the Trayvon Martin case. Trayvon Martin, another unarmed teen, was senselessly victimized and killed for being a perceived threat in the state of Florida. His killer, George Zimmerman, who asserted the legal defense of "Stand Your Ground" was found not guilty of his murder. The high profile case divided the nation in what would spark a national debate on the legal framework of "Stand Your Ground" and the terror and attack of unarmed black and brown people. While many initially felt helpless, the shooting of

85

Trayvon Martin, the use of "Stand Your Ground" as a legal defense, soon led to policy debates and the regular recording of incidents through the use of camera phones and video surveillance.

I am reminded of a very personal story that significantly affected me both personally and professionally. On Friday, November 23, 2012, an unarmed young man by the name of Jordan Davis lost his life. Jordan was parked outside a gas station with friends, in Jacksonville, Florida, just a few hours away from where I grew up and in the state of Florida, now my district while working for Senator Nelson. The teens were listening to music when approached by Michael Dunn, a patron of the gas station, who pulled up in the parking space next to them. Dunn requested that they turn the music down. The teens agreed to do so, but shortly after they decided to turn the music back up. Dunn began firing rounds into the SUV where the teens were sitting. Dunn stated that he was forced to defend himself by opening fire and alluded to the fact that he saw a gun. The investigation revealed that the teens did not have a gun in their possession and that Jordan Davis, senselessly lost his life. Dunn was charged with first-degree murder and three counts of attempted first-degree murder.

Soon after, Jordan Davis' mother, Lucy McBath, became an advocate for gun control reform. She embarked upon a connection with the mothers of the twenty victims from the Sandy Hook Elementary School Massacre in Newtown, Connecticut who banned together through an organization called Moms Demand Action for Gun Sense in America. This step for Lucy McBath initiated the process of accruing political currency from which to rally for change.

While I was working in the Senate, Mrs. McBath came to meet with me as part of her work with Moms Demand Action.

She is an extraordinary person, who has taken her pain and grown very politically sophisticated. Before her son's untimely death, she was a flight attendant and had no prior political experience. However, her courage and determination to advocate on behalf of her son for gun reform knew no limits. Today, she is a nationally recognized anti-gun violence activist. Mrs. McBath and has won the Democratic primary runoff for the Sixth Congressional District in the State of Georgia. Identifying and responding to a political need can result in becoming a voice for an important policy issue such as gun control. Lucy McBath's evolution from an everyday citizen with no political experience, to activist to a Congressional candidate, is an excellent example of women cultivating political currency.

Forward March

There is no reason valid enough for women not to be involved as leaders and at all levels, and by all means in the political process. Leadership is not limited to one form or fashion. It can and should be executed from many different vantage points. If we consider everything that we do as a leadership task, we become more enlightened and strategic about our actions. When women are in the room as active participants, specific sexist comments will not be made freely, and political positions will include the perspective of fifty-one percent of the population.

Let us take a step further. I would offer that some of the most influential women are not officially involved in politics. They are the wives and daughters of elected officials. Women have far more influence, but they do not get the recognition or the credit. Today marks a time when women can recognize and use their influence to impact our country and our world in ways unimaginable. We must ask ourselves how to achieve this end, and we must generate responses that open doors of opportunity.

Do What You Are Good At

If you are not a speechwriter, don't force yourself to write a speech. Discover your power in another arena. An impact can be made through action; I do mean any action. Take action by raising money, supporting others and making phone calls. Every woman is a subject matter expert. If you are a nurse, you have the power, education, and credibility to speak up about health care. If you are an educator, you can speak on funding for schools and classroom initiatives. If you are a housewife, you can teach everyone to multitask. Start where you are, with what you have. Find your niche and get up and get moving!

Act Now

You don't have to wait to get engaged. Leverage your influence by engaging in discussions in your home. Research topics that are important to you, and choose topics that affect you directly or ones that you believe are in need of attention. Start by creating awareness within your circles. While many feel as though discussing politics should be off limits, it is a way to ensure that those around you are knowledgeable of political issues and political candidates. Encourage the right to vote and the importance of voting for candidates who advocate for like-minded issues. An open and honest discussion is a way to influence people towards the desired outcome. Even if you do not recognize these actions as powerful, they are indeed affecting change. If you feel that your engagement so energizes you, then you might want to run for office.

Cut the Check

You may not consider yourself to be savvy regarding political fundraising and contributing, but if you have ever heard the saying, "put your money where your mouth is," then you would recognize the importance of lending your financial support towards supporting or opposing issues that you have a personal interest in changing. This also is true of candidates. When you contribute, you feel more invested in the outcomes. Candidates do not always fund their campaigns or initiatives; in fact, they typically encourage several people to help them raise money and make contributions for their race or ballot initiative. Doing so builds support for the candidate across the community or the district. A well-known adage tells us that money talks.

Educate Yourself

Education is free. Ignorance is expensive. As women, we have a responsibility to align ourselves with reliable data. What we desire to materialize can't just be based solely on emotional circumstances. There is evidence to support every issue, and technology is available to access unlimited information through research.

As women, we have more power than we know and most certainly more than social constraints would have us to believe. We can mobilize; we can multitask with the best of them. We can change the world, if and only if, we are willing to take action.

Building Alliances

If I am working with a member in Congress who is of a different political affiliation, it is still possible that we have a common goal, contingent upon what the issues at hand are. We do not have to agree on everything. If there are things we can work on together, it is best to look for those areas of commonality. Sometimes the greater goal, the final bill passage is more important than fighting about every single point. Some points of contention upon deeper review do not have anything to do with the actual issue being debated. Sometimes, the battle is won in peace and resolve, if that is a possibility. I may agree with a colleague about the Dakota Pipeline, but I may disagree on the benefits of Obamacare. Does this mean that we cannot work together? This could be a way to open the door to a broader conversation. It is possible that future open doors result from working harmoniously in previous scenarios. American politics and the ideal of leadership constitute finding ways to work together to foster change. Very few policy changes are accomplished by fiat or unilaterally; however, most things require a majority of votes of some means. For example, agency rules require a public comment period because our American government is set up for people to participate, collectively and collaboratively. Having one person who makes all the decisions and others who retreat to their perspectives will lead to counterproductivity in all facets. The actual exercise of leadership is about discovering commonality.

E. SHE Wins

ii.   Creating Pathways in the Political Process

If a path that leads to our intended destination does not exist, we are charged with the responsibility of creating one. For women, pathways that lead to the political process are not always flanked by opened doors but are without question accessible. Relentless pioneers and visionaries have overcome many barriers, and although there are some left to conquer, we must continue to chart our courses while doing so. The first step towards this end is examining everything that stands in the way of women leading. Identifying such barriers produces a competitive edge for change and the evolution to create the future that we so desire.

Perception

Let's address the elephant in the room. Even though women have run for the highest office that exists since 1872, there is still the lingering perception that women are not capable, ill-equipped, or too emotional to handle power. Victoria Woodhull is rarely mentioned, but she should be recognized for seeking the highest political office before women had the right to vote. Hillary Clinton had skill and expertise for days, yet her candidacy was resisted by men and women alike. Some might say that she comes off as "too strong," "too masculine," and "not needing a man". For some, she is perceived as threatening. However, by winning the Democratic nomination, she demonstrated that countless women and men recognize the value of strength in the face of opposition and adversity and power in the ability to exercise compassion and humility. Women are endowed with the ability to assume the responsibility as the givers of life, and they bask in the dual leadership and submissiveness that accompany the act of caring for another human being. Women are created to both lead and follow. How else can we explain the concept of motherhood? It is a mysterious phenomenon, but this dual skill set can be impactful in the political space.

Why do some feel the need to place women who lead in a box? The way in which we perceive women who lead can either be categorized as innovative or catastrophic. Perhaps one of the most startling revelations is that a great deal of the criticism for women in leadership comes from other women. By contrast, how often do we see men criticizing the leadership ability of the leaders that their respective party has selected? Some might say that the chain of command in direct leadership is more familiar among men.

Women are capable of bringing about change through advocacy, office and creating avenues of awareness for every ear that will hear. The perceptions that plague women who dare to lead is distracting and disengaging. Consider the possibilities for change if we challenge ourselves to denounce the perception that women leading is a moot point. Consider a world where women lead, nurture, cultivate, guide, teach and follow. That is my definition of the "American Dream." Women know as well as anyone that public service is a sacrifice of time, money and resources; it is a labor of love. What I know to be true is that when SHE WINS, everyone wins!

iii.   **Opening Doors for Other Women – Mentorship, Promotion, and Provision of Opportunities for Advancement**

The year was 1990, and I was preparing to walk through the threshold of the auditorium of Smith College. I was naive, yet an excited first-year student and my heart, mind, and soul were filled with the expectation of what could be. The auditorium was filled with young women from all backgrounds. At that moment, I felt a sense of camaraderie with the women there, even though I had only seen a few faces that were vaguely familiar. Perhaps it was because we would all eventually become the class of 1994.

As the faculty filled the auditorium, a petite lady in a floral dress emerged at the forefront. Although I did not know who she was, the room was silent, and her demeanor demonstrated that she had a message of substance for the crowd, who like me, found themselves embracing the moment in time.

As she approached the microphone, she offered the traditional salutations and greetings that are customary before every speech is delivered. Still unaware of who she was, her words overflowed into a pool of inspiration, and then she said…"Smith women can do anything….If you want to fly a plane, you can. If you want to start a company, you can. If you want to be an orchestra conductor, you can. Smith women can do anything." This unequivocal degree of confidence claimed my full attention, and I became fully engrossed in exploring the possibilities that the mantra, "Smith women can do anything," encompassed.

Now, I understood who she was and what she meant to the school. Mary Maples Dunn, President of Smith College, had ignited a flame deep within me. I am confident that I can speak for the rest of the room when I say that her words became the wind beneath our wings for excellence. The auditorium erupted in cheering. She also showed us at that moment just how potent the words of a woman, who existed to speak life into the spirit of another woman, could prove to be.

I never forgot that day, and I will never stray away from the lessons that the experience taught me. Mentorship, leadership, and sisterhood are unprecedented keys to our need to heal, restore, inspire and empower one another. We are charged with being the keeper of the heart of every woman. We are just like the women in the Smith College Auditorium. Mentors are for moments, seasons, but not necessarily for a lifetime. They are there to help you get to your next step. If you are reading this book, I hope that something in it will encourage you to count me among your mentors. Our similarities outweigh our differences, and because of this, we can offer our support.

A Push in the Right Direction

For every step that we ascend, it is good to recognize the value in lending a helping hand. My platform of support was enhanced by being in the presence of women who poured wisdom into my mind and substance into my spirit. I have always been blessed to stand firmly upon support from my grandmother, my mother, my aunts and the amazing women in my community. I have known mentorship for as long as I can remember.

Their tutelage was filled with messages of reassurance and confidence. Their whispers of confirmation inspired me to feel safe as I took leaps of faith amidst uncertainty. I've recognized the strength and the ability to denounce the ideology of failure at all costs. I learned how to have my own back, and I knew that I was not in the world alone. My mentors were with me in spirit and in truth.

As I got older, I recognized the value in casting my net wider and developing such relationships with ladies with whom I shared professional core values. Doing so has proven to be one of the single most powerful acts of my lifetime. Engaging, exchanging and supporting like-minded women create an energy that cannot be tamed. This alchemy is what we all know as mentorship. I have been blessed to share time, energy and space with confident women who are also political mentors. I'd like to tell you about three of them.

When I was in high school, I met a woman by the name of Margaret Boonstra. Mrs. Boonstra is a retired Foreign Service Officer. She has lived in South America, married a much older diplomat and is a Democrat who enjoys fundraising, canvassing and helping others get out to vote. I give her credit for recruiting me to Smith College. She too has a love of politics, and I learned from her that women can be both politically and family oriented. She has been a role model and a friend to me for the better part of my adult life.

Later in college, I had a mentor named Carol Thompson Cole. Carol was an alumna of Smith College, a newlywed, and at the time she was the Vice President for Governmental Affairs at then RJR Nabisco. Carol was the former City Manager for Mayor Marion Barry in Washington, D.C. She was from Virginia, and she was also on the Smith College Board of Trustees. In her, I saw someone that I could admire, respect and emulate. We even shared some similarities in resemblance.

I met her during my sophomore year. I was just nineteen years old. She was on campus frequently, in connection with her Board of Trustee meetings and responsibilities. I took advantage of every opportunity to send her thank you notes and write her letters to share my thoughts and goals and to seek her advice and counsel. I inquired about everything from internships to the courses that I should take. She helped me to make sense of it all. She was a responsive, sounding board. The fact that someone who was so busy and so successful in her own right took the time to call me, a college student, blew me away. From a confidence standpoint, Carol helped me to fill in the question marks. If I believed that I could do anything, she would help me fill in the blanks as I decided what I wanted to do next. I admired her for so many reasons and kept in touch with her throughout my college years. She set the standard for how I would later treat my mentees. Carol will always be another poignant reminder of the power of sowing seeds into your fellow sisters.

A Fresh Perspective

After I graduated from Harvard, I moved back to Florida. A chance meeting would place me in position to cross paths with Yolanda Cash Jackson. Yolanda is an African American, a million dollar, high-powered lobbyist based in South Florida. She is brilliant, down to earth, and has killer business acumen. She was an attorney, turned lobbyist, who began working in government relations after graduating from law school. Her managing partner gave her freedom and space to build her own arm of the firm, which led to unprecedented success. Our exchanges led me to regard her as a mentor and colleague, and our relationship has resulted in a friendship that has lasted for decades. She is one of those people that you don't talk to all of the time, but when you do, she has such great wisdom and advice that it lasts you until the next confab. Her personality is so much fun, but her wit leaves me in awe of her insightfulness.

Furthermore, her political instincts are second to none. Over the years, I have also come to trust her as a great confidant. Having a mentor that you trust is invaluable. Knowing that there is someone who can speak or advocate on your behalf if someone is criticizing you is so meaningful.

Today, I do all that I can do demonstrate through merit and deed that I support my fellow sisters. I can offer support by reviewing resumes, writing recommendations, taking phone calls and performing other supportive tasks. Kindness and sisterhood were passed along to me, and with all that I have, I pay it forward just as acts of kindness were gifted unto me.

Part III:
Woman

"Dear women, you are not intimidating, you are beautiful."

-Stephanie Mickle-

AS WOMEN, WE are builders of souls and gatekeepers of hearts. As givers and nurturers, we hold up this world. To be a woman is to be one with all humanity. At times, we endure difficulty, hardship and remain upbeat. I am ever inspired by the countless women who personify the sentiment of beauty for ashes.

We, as women, are valuable. We are called to embrace our very essence of femininity and still blaze new trails, which illuminate examples of excellence for those girls and women who come after us. In understanding and recognizing our worth, we must also find the value in unsubscribing to societal imposed standards of who and what we should be, which does not align with our individual highest and best selves. It is up to us to take pathways that lead to success. In doing so, we maintain our own integrity.

Excellence demands that we release the baggage that often weighs us down. This means alleviating the dead weight of others' expectations, past failures, childhood trauma, hurt from strained relationships and even childhood memories that do not speak to the women that we desire to become. This self-affirming process opens the doors for healing. We must seek to be and remain healed and to be whole, engaging with life and allowing ourselves to discover the voice within that we may not have known or may not have remembered existed. If we are whole as women, we can impart much-needed balance and all with being right with the world.

The by-product of a woman who is whole is a community positively affected, uplifted and empowered. When a woman wins, we all win. Men win, women win, children win, and those who do not identify with a gender win. Countless statistics demonstrate the value of investing in women and girls. This explains why a great deal of funding is allocated towards youth empowerment programs for girls. When women and girls invest in their communities, they lead and contribute in ways that yield better policy outcomes for all. So much is rooted in the creativity of a woman and her disposition in the world.

A. The Divine Influence and the Measure of a Woman

i. God

As a young girl, I grew up amidst a very strict Baptist religious background, which meant spending a great deal of time at church or church-related events with my siblings. Our mother's influence was very much a part of this aspect of life. My father was supportive, and for our family, the establishment of spiritual traditions was of great importance. Someone in high school once gave me a card that proclaimed: "You see God in everything." The card was affirming in many ways and allowed me to make meaningful connections to the teachings, beliefs and religious traditions that I had learned in church.

My grandfather would kneel publicly and pray when he was well into his 80's. My mom would join prayer groups, and she encouraged others to do the same. Prayer is one of those communication tools that just seemed like a normal part of life for me. I pray for all sorts of reasons, big and small. As an attorney and counselor, I pray when making decisions and giving legal advice. I was always moved to pray as a student when completing my assignments and as a leader for wisdom and continued strength. I pray to seek God's direction before I make the next move or resolve to take action in a given situation. No matter how great or small, prayer is a way to connect with God and seek direction, divine guidance and express gratitude. I had prayed throughout college and graduate studies, and even as a baby lawyer at Akerman Senterfitt, but when I began working for Senator

Nelson, who is a devout Christian, I became even more convinced about the power of prayer. My legal training tells me that as human beings, any one person can only see part of a scenario. She may have facts and details, but they often just show a partial picture. In fact, in a courtroom, it takes a jury of several people to determine, based on the evidence, what happens in a case. It is because, on a fundamental level, we know that people do not know everything, and we do not have all the answers. The flurry of activity and movement on Capitol Hill, one of the highest heights of power, was fast-paced and ever-changing. Everyone there wanted something: from advocacy groups to staffers and lobbyists, people wanted to advance his or her agendas. As a staffer, one of my responsibilities was to attend to all of those requests and to make recommendations to Senator Nelson about what he should consider. I knew without question that I was giving my best advice and counsel, but I also recognized that I was a human being, who did not have 360-degree vision. It was inevitable that there would be factors for consideration about a situation that I might not be aware of. Even in instances after I had done all of the due diligence and written what I felt to be my best memorandum or briefing, there was still a possibility that he would get a phone call with additional information, or that someone would grab him at an event and put a bug in his ear. There were always factors outside of my control that could potentially influence his decision or redirect his attention. My prayer request was to ask God to reveal to Senator Nelson anything that he should know that was outside of my realm of awareness. I prayed that God would reveal all of the information needed to make a sound decision: a decision that would positively affect people and bring the most good for the people of Florida and the United States.

Morality is a great reason to get involved or to stay engaged in the political process. An essential part of public policy requires that we ask ourselves if we are doing what is best for those we serve. For example, am I considering those in need of advocacy in this financial industry regulation or housing legislation? Keeping these sentiments at the forefront helps maintain the moral fiber that can break down in politics. There are situations where doing what is fundamentally and morally right become the reason that you stay in the game because it is easy to get frustrated. Some may think that a law will never change or that their work has no impact. Many will wonder if their advocacy on behalf of a particular issue like gun control will ever be addressed in a meaningful way by Congress. No matter the issue, there will come a time during your political journey when you have doubts. These are the times when you have to remember why you got involved in the first place. These are the times when it is good to consult with God for divine influence. There are also times when we as women innately know that we should take action.

In politics, there is backstabbing, back riding, lies, deception, gamesmanship, and everything else that you can name. People can be laser-focused on their respective agendas, and God can often be left out of the equation. The whole notion of asking ourselves "What Would Jesus Do" in a given situation is not always at the forefront. It might not be a considered topic at all. Operating under this level of scrutiny and in an environment such as this can be taxing. America is experiencing turbulent times, political fights, the rise of extremist views and more, and you may be questioning why bother? Others considering getting involved may wonder if they can sustain under such levels of intensity. Taking time to reflect and to ask these questions will prove to be effective ways to gain the clarity that is so desperately needed, no matter whether you are considering local, state, national or international opportunities in politics.

Let's consider a recent policy development that was particularly troubling for many women that I know. You may have even seen it as a clarion call for action. The Trump Administration enacted an immigration policy which separated migrant parents and their children at the Southwestern border of the United States as a purported deterrent to illegal immigration. Among the many disheartening things that occurred was several children were separated from their parents and taken to different parts of the United States of America. The children were placed in cages, and their parents were charged money to talk on the phone to their children. As mothers, sisters, daughters and the givers of life, such actions should be offensive to each of us. Any woman who sees a scenario such as this would likely be moved to tears at the prospect of their child being taken away because of a decision made by a government that does not protect the child's best interest. This action prompted allegations of abuse and neglect. This is not to say that men do not have the same reactions; many do. As women, this is the type of policy change that should resonate at the deepest levels of our hearts.

When you consider how to get involved and where to use your gifts and talents to be impactful, I challenge you to discuss it with God. He can tell you where your strengths are, intercede to help you to meet the right people, and even place you in position to learn what you need to know to lead. Some may think that such details are excessive. I will leave that to you to decide for yourself. I invite you to note that the measure of a woman is in her divine ability to be productive and creative. I invite you to bring about change for the betterment of our families, communities and the world. Doing so requires insight and action. Prayer and the cultivation of a spiritual relationship are necessities in utilizing both effectively. We need God in life, in relationships, in work and in politics.

ii.   Health and Self Care

There is nothing selfish about caring for self. The adage that you cannot pour from an empty cup rings true. In today's fast-paced society, we often neglect our own needs to meet the expectations of others. We consistently place deadlines and approval of people, coupled with the desire to produce, at the forefront of our objectives.

While working on Capitol Hill, I worked up to fourteen hours a day, and I kept two smartphones: one for work and one for personal use. I was connected to the internet, my email and various news alerts. I read an average of eight newspapers daily, and I either listened to or watched the news all day long from the television on my desk. In fact, by the time the evening news came on, it was no longer news to me, as I had been attentive to the news all day. Doing so helped me to stay current, maintain my competitive edge, be prepared for national and international developments, and it gave me a thrill because I love politics. I felt what I was doing professionally was important.   Sometimes, I failed to unplug and take a break, and my life became out of balance.   After working tirelessly on Capitol Hill for almost six years, which is twelve years in regular job time because of the pace, we like to say, I decided to embark upon a self-imposed six month sabbatical in Houston, Texas to shift my focus. My life slowed down considerably, and my priorities were different. To many, Texas feels like a different country. Being there helped me to focus on other aspects of my health and myself. In the state of Texas, there is great emphasis on God, family, and money. It was different from D.C. where government and politics are concentrated and permeate most areas of life. It is interesting that when you move into an environment that embodies a new set of priorities, you see ways that you can develop your personal goals and objectives.

I started by detaching myself from the twenty-four-hour news cycle. In Houston, there were days when I reached a point that I did not watch the news at all, which was a completely different tact from my typical life. I began working out with a personal trainer and shifted a great deal of my attention to my niece and nephew, who were very young at the time. In their presence, I got to practice and connect to my maternal side. Before that time, I was not even sure if I could be a good mom because I had not had children of my own. However, I quickly fell in love with them and with the maternal side of myself. Houston also reminded me to get back to myself and to engage in acts of self-care. Participating in activities such as painting my nails, getting facials, taking naps, taking walks, exercising, meditation, yoga and journaling became a part of my usual routine. Simple, yet powerful self-care activities such as having a nice, long, hot bath and a cup of tea, writing and enjoying happy times with loved ones can seem like luxuries when you are spending so much time reaching that next height or accomplishment.

When you work at a fast pace and are out of balance, over time, even vacations cannot silence the noise. A vacation is nice, but you know that at the end of it, you will be returning to the same grind and the same obligations. In the workspace, I believe that it becomes imperative for us to take a step back to be completely clear about our use of time, priorities and objectives. After you have pushed hard on something, a political race, a legislative ballot initiative, or your career, you should take a sabbatical, and make no apologies for doing so. Even if you have a family, plan for it financially and do it. Make no excuses to yourself or others about why it is necessary.

Colleges and universities have it right when they encourage professors to go on sabbatical. Sabbaticals refresh and help you nurture yourself, your loved ones and to be clear about what you want to do next. This is how we can all develop both personally and professionally. A sabbatical presents itself as an opportunity to ask yourself if you have grown past the last opportunity that you took on? Taking time to consider if you want to continue in the same vein that you have been working in and reflecting on life decisions can be priceless. Analyzing the lessons that you have learned in the process can be a building block to your next initiative. Also, writing these sentiments down can reveal a great deal about your innermost thoughts that can be obscured amongst the daily routines. For me, detox came in the form of a sabbatical. When you are in need of a break and contemplating your next move, consider making the time to take a sabbatical to pause, reflect and to gain perspective on where you are headed next.

iii.   Love Lives

For me, love and dating have always ebbed and flowed. Like most successful women, I have had to determine the best ways to manage my social life and my personal life. I believe this is a consideration that many women, driven to lead, encounter. There have been times when I have prioritized my love life and doing so made me happy. There have been times when I prioritize my career, and in those moments, doing so also made me happy, primarily when there was just not a love connection with a man that was also sparked in my life.

I believe that we are meant to be in relationships with one another. It has been said that love is even a superpower. When you do have love in your life, it boosts you to be better in other areas. It is affirming to find someone who desires to assist you in your journey of growth and progress. If you have a person who positively supports and influences you, love can be one of the most beautiful aspects of life.

In dating and romance, I was a late bloomer by most accounts. My parents instructed me to prioritize education and that everything else was secondary. They told me to study, and make good grades, and that boys would come later. I was not allowed to date or wear makeup until the age of sixteen, and I can count on one hand the number of dates that I went on during high school. When I attended college, I was free to make choices for myself, and one of the first was to start dating regularly. I enjoyed the courtship process, and I learned a lot about myself during that time. As you embark on your political journey, be sure to make time for love and romance. It will make the highs and the lows of civic engagement much more enjoyable.

Many women do not know how to navigate both worlds. I have even heard instances where some men have said that some women do not know how to separate their work skills from their life skills. While this can be a fair criticism in some instances, all women have the right to be true to themselves. Inauthenticity does not lend itself to stability or success. That said, navigating love, leadership and politics require intentionality. The things that we choose to prioritize determine the outcomes of the relationships that we enjoy.

iv.   Life Balance – Hospitality, Finances, and Community

Life Balance

As women, we are built to do multiple things at a time. This can be good for efficiency. I developed a mindfulness meditation practice as a way to maintain balance while I was working in the Senate. Mindfulness teaches you to focus on one thing like breathing or walking as the most important thing that you are doing at a given period. For example, mindfulness can be practiced while washing the dishes. You remain focused on that activity, to the exclusion of everything else, until you have completed it, and then you move to the next task and do the same thing. It sounds painfully simple, but it is more challenging than one might expect. Focusing on the moment is a valuable and powerful safeguard against overstimulation and stress that results from trying to juggle everything all at once. We function best when settled and not when our minds are convoluted with excessive thoughts and our bodies are on the brink of physical exhaustion and our emotions are overwhelmed. When we become entangled in our emails, phone calls, meetings, travel, client deliverables, family and personal commitments, projects and everything else, it is possible to be engaged in something twenty four hours per day.

Believe it or not, it helps your mind and your body when you can step away from one area of your life and do something different. There are scientific studies to prove it. If I have spent fourteen hours working on a Monday, which can be typical, that is a clear signal that I do not need to spend fourteen hours working the next day. For me, excessive hours at work can be a clear indicator that I need to find a way to adjust the allocation of my time and resources so that I can remain at my best and maintain my competitive edge. Balance is imperative to being your best self in politics and in life. I believe that it is also necessary to take into consideration that there are seasons that we will need to put in more hours. The goal is to ensure that it does not become a way of life. When this level of production becomes standard, we can get tired, frustrated, or feel as if a piece of us is getting neglected. In the long run, being out of balance leads to health issues, depression, strained relationships and even the loss of relationships. The noble attempt to balance all that we are tasked with can be taxing. However, revitalization in the company of those whom we share similarities and those with whom we desire to share time, space and energy can be an excellent antidote.

Community

An extension of hospitality is to build community. We can develop friendships by working within our churches, supporting our children's athletic teams, contributing to charities and philanthropic efforts or volunteering with local community organizations. Every action that we take to share our time, resources and energy to assist or uplift someone or something outside of our homes helps to build community. The more we work hand in hand with those whom we share and engage, the more we establish a rapport. This is a possibility, and it can become a reality in small towns, big cities, and communities. We are all extremely busy, which can cause us to focus more of our attention on our own needs, and at times neglect the needs of our neighbors and communities. Building friendships, working, giving and playing, side by side in our communities can also lead to an excellent understanding and tolerance of the life experiences of other people. It helps us to hear one another and to understand perspectives that are different from our own. Building a community is something that we can do well when we are intentional about doing so. Joining online communities and sharing on social media platforms are fun activities and can be valuable ways to express views, but they are not a substitute for actual human interactions and engagements within our local communities. By taking the time to engage organically, we emphasize that maintaining a sense of community is essential.

Hospitality

Nurturing relationships begin and end with our ability to make others feel welcome in our space. Encouraging and engaging can be phenomenal ways to recharge. People respond well when you show through your actions that your doors are opened. Inviting people into your space commands that it is orderly. Many might not consider the fact that a tidy home can assist in maintaining order in every other area of your life. I love having a clean house and a clean office. A clean home is especially refreshing for me and presents a place of refuge for me as well as those that I choose to invite into my space. Order helps us to be more effective as human beings. If you have children, you have probably noticed that they respond differently to a clean house compared with a messy house. If you teach them to keep their spaces, their rooms and their toys, orderly, and you make an effort to maintain a clean home, everyone is a lot happier. Like it or not, I believe this to be a fact. A clean house and a clean workspace allow us to function more effectively. You may know a person -- or be that person yourself -- that people love coming to visit because they know that there will be something delicious to eat, something tasty to drink and a pleasant, welcoming environment with good company.

Finances

Women have a tremendous impact on the direction of finances in a household. Advertisers market their products to women because they recognize that women likely execute the purchase of products and the selection of brands and services. The wife, mother or woman in the household often sets the tone for the family's spending choices. She is the one who chooses the right laundry detergent, determines the car that best suits the needs of the family and even selects brands of food that the family eats. These decisions and their impact spread beyond our homes; they dictate practices and policies made by major industries in our country.

As women, we embody perspectives on our family's finances that open doors for conversations on every entity that impacts the family. The financial views of women are critical to the decisions that are made on healthcare, childcare, and education on the local and national levels. When Obamacare was being debated, some asked why the country needed to be responsible for the cost of health care under a single-payer system. Ultimately, that proposal did not advance.

Furthermore, some did not see medical expenses such as birth control or mammograms as priorities. Decision makers failed to acknowledge the impact on a family's ability to sustain in the wake of an unexpected pregnancy or illness resulting from the lack of screening. If women do not have mammograms on a regular basis, the chances increase for the development of a disease that has been proven to be costly and in some instances fatal. Screenings that can lead to continued health or early detection should not be optional. An unexpected illness in a household can pose a significant financial burden on the family's income. Operating from a premise of prevention rather than treatment is meaningful for individual families as well as the country. Women, and many men in Congress, readily pointed out those financial implications and ultimately the provisions for mammograms and birth control along with other preventative care were included in the final bill.

Likewise, when women decide to financially support a candidate or a cause, they make a bold statement that they believe the issues that the candidate stands for are essential. This act also demonstrates that women are serious about public policy issues, and they recognize the value in holding candidates or elected officials accountable for decisions that are made. Society does not always categorize women as significant contributors, but being a financial contributor to issues and candidates is very important. I urge you to consider the continuance of pushing the envelope through contributing money in support of better public policy. Women can be impactful in all areas in the financial decision-making process for their homes and in the discussions surrounding public policies and practices. Women make considerable contributions to political campaigns and charitable organizations. The ability to give and contribute to causes and issues is a factor that women should continue to consider when managing household finances. It helps everyone when women leverage their buying and contributing power, and it gives women a voice in the prioritization of the causes, candidates, and the entities that they decide to support.

When we give our best to ourselves, take accountability for our actions, and invite the divine influence into our affairs, we are best equipped to function in the political space and in life. In my view, they are interrelated. The way in which we relate to others and serve as stewards of our varied personal, human, and financial resources reflects our strengths and various skill sets. When women consider community, hospitality, finances, love, self-care, health and God, and celebrate where we are performing well, as well as the areas that could benefit from further development, we lead by example. As women, we all have places in our lives where we can grow and places where we can cheer. Having and maintaining balance in the various aspects of our lives plays a role in the extent to which we can influence, impact, and be of service in public policy and other areas of society.

B. The Superwoman Syndrome

i. Connecting to Masculinity to Misalignment

The Superwoman Syndrome begins with noble intentions. We want to be the best sisters, mothers, wives, employees, and employers. We strive to be the most accomplished, most celebrated, wealthiest, happiest, most loving, most spiritually connected, the most in every other facet of excellence that can be imagined. Each of these aspirations is ambitious and positive. Each is food for the soul and places us in a position to nurture others. As women, we are innately composed to care for and nurture others. The Superwoman Syndrome happens when we believe that we can do all of these things simultaneously.

Women are and have always been ready, willing and able to conquer the world. I do not dispute the premise that a woman can do anything that a man can do, within reason -- physical strength notwithstanding. The question that we must pose to ourselves is: Do we want to do everything that men do? Are there tasks that are reserved only for a specific gender? Our individual preferences should drive our answers to these questions and the great debate surrounding gender roles. Our priorities can and should determine the opportunities that we pursue. What and how we choose to present to the world should be as personalized as our fingerprints.

ii. Over Functioning and Being in Charge of Everything

In many ways, the overarching messaging towards women is flanked with undertones that glorify the notion of having it all. Women are encouraged to have it all and having it all is often likened to perfection. In many ways, women are led to believe that -- in the absence of the perfect house, car, husband, 2.5

children, or the ideal job -- they are not worthy of societal accolades. We have even been encouraged to subscribe to superficial definitions of perfection in our appearance. We can find ourselves consumed with striving for perfection such that we become imbalanced. Regardless of our decisions regarding the roles that we assume, the fact remains that time is finite. It is a limited resource. We become less productive when we sleep and eat less. Our effectiveness is significantly diminished when we neglect to care for ourselves while chasing societal imposed standards of what we should do and who we should be. We work to do and to be more and often disregard the need for self-care and balance. This can lead to misalignment in so many aspects of our lives.

When we perform multiple tasks at a high level for long periods of time, we sacrifice more than we realize. In these instances, we don't make time for ourselves. It is possible that we do not eat or exercise regularly or that we miss out on time to pray. During these times, we may not communicate as effectively with loved ones or stay in touch with friends. If you find that the twenty-four hours of the day do not include time for you, it is easy to fall victim to the Superwoman Syndrome.

In my life, I still have to be mindful of the potential to fall victim to the Superwoman Syndrome. I recognize that even in doing the things that I love such as running my business, doing fun projects around the house, traveling to new places or composing this book, it is possible. Once, I was reminded of it when I passed out in a public restroom at the grocery store. It was embarrassing to have the paramedics called, equipment brought out and people watching me and wondering what was going on. I had fainted and was unaware of my dehydration. Consumed with work and the day to day, I had not used any of the hours from my day to drink enough water. This could have been prevented if I had made sure that I was getting the necessary hydration for the day. This level of dehydration did not just happen from one day and a little lack of attention to myself; it happened over time. I simply forgot to drink enough water and underestimated how much water my body needed. Although drinking enough water is a very simple thing that does not require much effort, it can pose a problem if ignored. My case was proof of the fact that I needed to be more considerate of myself amidst all of the tasks that I was executing on a daily basis.

Our health and well-being require us to determine what spaces we should operate effectively in and what areas we should allow others to consume. It requires that we stay in our lanes. Despite our best efforts and most honorable intentions, we cannot fix it or make it better for everyone without significant cost to ourselves. Learning to classify all of our actions with their associated costs, provides excellent insight and clarity and keeps us free from the Superwoman Syndrome. What we choose to allocate our energy, time, money, emotions and resources to should only be those things that we prioritize.

Do We Need to Wear the Superwoman Cape?

Discovering balance is the ultimate goal. I am someone who prioritizes everything that is on my plate, with a line of demarcation. Anything that falls above the line gets my attention. Anything that falls below the line gets delegated or declined. I have learned to use the word "no". Sometimes it can be hard to deny requests made of you, but when an opportunity, event, person, place or thing does not serve us well or align with what we have prioritized and are working to accomplish, it is best that we do. We must learn to say "no" early and as often as needed. For me, this has been an evolution. I was raised to be a good girl who said "yes" and who followed the leaders. I was compliant. This way of thinking serves you well in particular social structures, although I do not believe that it helps you to be the most well rounded, whole, human being. We must learn to be content with not doing everything. Sometimes the most important thing that you have to do in a day is to sit with a friend who needs you or enjoy a cup of tea with your feet up to recharge. There are times when the most important thing that you will need to do in a day is to be still, and that is okay. Being a superwoman does not align with the recognition that there are only twenty-four hours in the day. Although they all belong to you, taking note of how many you give to others helps you to grasp just how few a superwoman gives to herself. It has been said that you cannot pour from an empty pitcher. Even superheroes must recharge.

A Special Note about Being a Black Woman and the Superwoman Syndrome

We are seeing more and more Nike commercials with strong women and girls on them. I love Serena Williams, the world-famous, award-winning, professional tennis player. She is by all accounts a strong black woman. She is beautiful, successful, happily married with a family, and she has a physique that many envy. Some would argue that being strong is a requirement for black women and other women of color, more so than women of other ethnicities and cultures. Why is this? I do not deny that most of the black women that I have met are strong. We have had to be. From a historical perspective, we have had our husbands and children sold away through slavery, and our families have been destroyed through legal and non-legal means. We have been victimized by rape and dealt with indignity and disrespect and devaluation. Only strength over time could survive such perils. All of those historical factors have at a minimum encouraged and/or forced black women to consider adopting a persona that believes that it can overcome any obstacle presented. Black women have personified the unwavering ability to survive and become numb if necessary to decry weakness at all costs.

Moreover, when faced with trauma or tragedy, we've had to suck it up, get over it and move on, without making space for the acknowledgment of the pain and the need for restoration and healing. For some, this is a coping mechanism, but for others, this way of thinking has become an identifier by which a person proclaims to the world that they are comfortable in their skin. The adoption of such behaviors can lead to unhealthy work ethics and unhealthy emotional places.

Conclusion

Excellence. Integrity. Professionalism.

As women, we have managed to thrive in every aspect of our lives. From overcoming obstacles to breaking down barriers, we serve, we follow, we lead. As we reflect upon our vast history, we can recognize tremendous strides made by and for women as guiding forces in the trajectory of our future endeavors.

We must never stop showing up prepared and ready to perform because our best policy outcomes require it. We must never stop believing in the power of change and our abilities to right what we believe to be wrong in our homes, communities and our country.

We must learn to tune out the noise that often fills our hearts with doubt. It is without question that we can sustain and command success at high levels. We must remain vigilant in the quest to discover our greatest purpose and resolve to do all that we are purposed to do.

We must recognize that when we lead, the world can and sometimes does label us as too aggressive or too masculine or too driven. We must denounce every word spoken that does not breathe the air of life into our existence. We must continue to dress the part, look the part, and to be friendly in the face of adversity. We are not inferior, aggressive, or angry. None of these sentiments speak to our innate abilities. We are conquerors and nurturers and creators forging new paths and innovative ideas and ways to make society better.

Moreover, as we desire to go to the top of the mountain that we so choose to climb, we must own every opportunity to get there. If you have read this book, I can glean that you are at least curious and at most compelled to make an impact in the political realm, as you should be. I implore you to always recognize the humanity in yourself and in others that can often be forgotten in the heat of a policy disagreement or political race.

Every face walking the earth has concerns about well being and family and safety and peace. We must stand upon these cornerstones as women in the political space, and at all costs. In doing so, I humbly request the following of you:

Build Allies

No person is an island. Breaking into the political process, or sustaining in any leadership capacity, requires the development of relationships with those who can be beneficial to your mission or vision. It is easy to see any frontrunner for an entity or organization, but we must never forget that it takes a village.

Seek Knowledge

There is a lot of misinformation in the air and confusion around what is truthful. We are bearing witness to an assault on the 1st Amendment.

Recognize that you are responsible for your own education and knowledge. Thirst for it. Not just in politics but in all things. There is power in being aware of the issues affecting your home, your community, your job, and your nation.

<u>Be Your Own Leader</u>

Develop your internal compass and, most importantly, your relationship with God. Ask yourself on a continual basis how you can impact society and remain true to your purpose.

Following the Leader means that you recognize your value, disposition in the world and take action to bring about positive change through your gifts and talents. I challenge you to take action. I challenge you to roll up your sleeves and work for change. I challenge you always to dig deep to discover the leader within you. She is capable, ready, willing and able to meet the challenge at hand. Follow the Leader. The leader is you. ♡

<u>Acknowledgements</u>

To God: You are so awesome every day, and I thank you for using me. I can't wait to see what You do next!

To Myself: thank you for keeping up with me and trusting the dreams and vision that God has placed inside! So glad I switched to plant-based lifestyle.

To my village: my parents, my brother, and sister, Amy and Stephan (the three amigos!), Aunt Ronnie, Grandma Catherine, my Ace Deuce Family, my Godparents, my aunts, uncles, cousins, extended, church and honorary families, a million and one thanks.

To the treasured friends whose paths crossed mine at Smith, Harvard Kennedy School and the University of Florida, thank you for the memories and for the world-class education in school and in life.

To the amazing people that I have met along the way, in different cities, jobs and life circumstances, thank you for your friendship, leadership, and mentorship along this journey.

To my sister friends, too many to name, thank you for helping me to be the best version of myself and the best woman that I can be.

To Gabrielle, Trey, Quentin, and Nakia: I love you to the moon and back. Keep making me proud.

To the last love of my life: counting the moments.

To Gainesville and DC: thank you for being my home, my foundation and my ground zero.

To my staff and interns at Mickle Public Affairs Agency: thank you for your dedication, hard work, and commitment on behalf of our customers and clients.

To my Nelson colleagues: thank you for your dedication and consistent commitment to making this country better.

To my publisher, 13th & Joan: Ardre, you and your team have been wonderful to work with.

To my photographer, Maya Darasaw, you have an amazing gift.

To my ancestors: Harry T. Moore, Grethel Moore, Frazier Moore, Grace Belton Mickle, Grace Ellis Mickle, and Andrew R. Mickle, thank you for the paths that each of you forged and for your commitments to a better life for me and future generations.

And finally, to those who will enter the political space or become leaders in their own right, Follow the Leader!

About the Author

STEPHANIE MICKLE is the CEO of Mickle Public Affairs Agency. Mickle Public Affairs Agency (MPA) is an elite full-service boutique public affairs agency. MPA expands and increases the influence of our clients so that they have an even greater reach by bringing to bear over twenty years of political, legal and business expertise drawing from a wide range of experiences and thought leadership in the areas of strategic communications, media, messaging, government relations, regulatory affairs, and public policy analysis.

Stephanie earned a Bachelor of Arts in Government from Smith College and a Master's in Public Policy from Harvard University. After graduating from Harvard, Stephanie began her full-time public policy career as the loan officer for the Florida Community Loan Fund, a statewide community development financial institution, where she was responsible for marketing and underwriting commercial real estate loans to nonprofit organizations that provide services in urban and rural communities.

From there she went on to law school at the University of Florida, and upon graduation, she practiced law with Akerman Senterfitt, a 500-attorney law firm where she represented businesses in both state and federal court in vendor disputes, product liability, and contractual claims. Stephanie also assisted businesses with various formation, licensing and regulatory issues, contract preparation, and review, lease agreement preparation and review and pre-litigation analysis. She is licensed to practice law before the United States Supreme Court and in the State of Florida.

In 2009, at the beginning of the Obama Administration, Stephanie began as a legislative counsel to U.S. Senator Bill Nelson of Florida, covering a broad variety of economic matters, including banking, insurance, small business, housing, and real estate. In 2011, she became General Counsel to Senator Nelson and in 2012, she was recognized by the Loop 21/lmpact DC as one of the 40 Under 40 Most Influential on Capitol Hill. Stephanie returned to the private sector in late 2014, where she launched her business.

Stephanie is a native of Gainesville, Florida. Stephanie is a lifelong politico and world changer. Stephanie is also a Woodrow Wilson Fellow and a proud member of Alpha Kappa Alpha Sorority, Inc. and Alfred Street Baptist Church in Alexandria, VA. In 2016, Stephanie served as the Co-Chair of the Legislative Committee for the National Bar Association, the nation's oldest voluntary bar association of over 66,000 lawyers, judges, law students and professors of color and in 2017, she served as the Director of the National Bar Association Political Action Committee.

Connect with Stephanie Mickle

Website: www.stephaniemickle.com
Facebook: @ stephaniemickle
Instagram: @ stephaniemickle1
Twitter: www.Twitter.com/StephanieMickle
LinkedIn: @ stephaniemickle

MICKLE PUBLIC AFFAIRS
A G E N C Y

Excellence. Integrity. Professionalism

"Increasing and Expanding the Reach of Our Clientele by
Delivering Expert Public Policy Results"

Mickle Public Affairs Agency
1629 K Street NW
Suite 300
Washington, DC 20006
(202) 403-2294 main

Notes:

_____

_____

_____

_____

_____

_____

_____

_____

_____

_____

_____

_____

_____

_____

_____

_____

_____

_____

_____

_____

_____

Notes:

Notes: